ABIDJAN
West Africa

```
PR 6060 .A224 A63 1990
Jackson, Dawson.
    Abidjan : West Africa : a
 poem
```

DATE DUE

BRODART, INC.   Cat. No. 23-221

Also by Dawson Jackson

LONG POEMS

All Is Never Said
The Ruin
Rome
New York
Delhi
Tropical Africa
Moments in Africa
The Elder Brother
Spring Beneath the Alps

MISCELLANIES

A Summer's Leisure
Remembrance of Venus
This Paradise
At Fifty
Young Women
Praises

PROSE WORKS

From This Foundation (novel)
A Primer of Necessary Belief (essay)
Against Destruction (essay)

ABIDJAN
WEST AFRICA

a poem

DAWSON JACKSON

With an Afterword by
MICHAEL SCHMIDT

Drawings and Cover by
ROSE ELLENBY

Lilstock Press
in association with Carcanet

First published in 1990 by
Lilstock Press
in association with
Carcanet Press Limited
208–212 Corn Exchange Buildings
Manchester M4 3BQ

Copyright © Dawson Jackson 1990

All rights reserved

British Library Cataloguing in Publication Data
Jackson, Dawson
    Abidjan : West Africa : a poem.
    I. Title
    821'.914

    ISBN 0-85635-887-8

Typeset by Paragon Photoset, Aylesbury
Printed in England by SRP Ltd, Exeter

Contents

PART ONE

Introduction		page 3
I	Breakfast	7
II	Through Treichville to the Bridge	25
III	On the Plateau	73
IV	Out to Adjamé	105

INTERLUDE

Amin Abdullah	139

PART TWO

I	Hôtel Haddad	165
II	Streets	205
III	Lagoon	231
IV	The Sea	253

AFTERWORD

by Michael Schmidt   307

PART ONE

INTRODUCTION

Free wings! One
Could

Fly out of life . . .

It is a long way
To the equator. Several hours'
Journey, by the
Aeroplane's new
Path in the sky – which

Mixes up for
Us, in that light blue
And blue black
Bowl, all latitudes and
Times of year, and night
And day, together.

I sit here and
Write of
Abidjan – where, a
Month back, I sat
And thought of

Here, of where
The life within
Me, my reality, my
Root, is. Up from

Which I
Grow, yet a
While, like
The autumn tendrils of the
Creeper on the wall – which smile

And shoot again
In the sun, forgetting
That winter in these
Northern latitudes with
Its knife comes

Soon, cuts
Down, so

That there may
Be space for
A new nursery
Of grandchildren
And the spring.

It is a short
Time, this
Eternity we live in.

*

My second grandchild is
Three today. A very
Young age. And yet a
Third is
Flying in – already

A full moon, in my
Daughter's belly. The world

Is filling up: as we
Empty out of
It, one
After another.

To be middle aged
As I am now is like
Living in
A war: one after
Another of those
I've known
Throughout my life
And love
Are shot down by
Death, picked off
By its bullet.

The round earth opens,
Open armed, to the
New blind

Visitor; and on
Those of us who
Have had
As it turns out
Their day

Turns its back.

Nightfall and
Dawn, together.

*

What is the point, the
Purpose, of
Our lives?

The sky gives back
No answer: we must find the
Answer in ourselves.

Here, there,
Everywhere, our
Purpose, the answer,
Is: it is a
Very simple
Nothing, which each
Holds in his hand.

And nothing that
We do is
Anything except in
The light
Of it: in its

Sunlight!

*

Turn over earth – back,
Time – through the cloud
Complexities and
Clock complications of the

Sky, to
Abidjan

And my hotel
Room there
In the heat.

I

BREAKFAST

1

Two stories up
In a corner of
The courtyard, this
Narrow veranda, outside
My hotel
Room door, is a

Passage: from
The head of the branching
Outside staircase to further
Shut up private
Cell rooms.

I camp out
On it
For breakfast: a pair

Of bananas
And a glass of tea
Or coffee – made from
My tap's
Questionable water, boiled up
With a small immersion heater
Plugged into that
Most convenient socket
One finds now
Everywhere where there is
Electric light (in place
Of the Africans'
Storm lanterns) for an
Electric razor.

From here I can
See out:
Down. My room (a cube

With loo, shower, hand basin,
Large bed, small
Table and a
Cupboard – in which
The black trousers that

I came in became
In a few days light
Cambridge blue
With mould) has

No windows: only
Holes punched in the
Back wall, at
A downward
Angle, and
Slats in the door
And shutters of
The unglazed
Windows, so
That air
Blows through,
When air stirs at
All, accompanied

By the sound (from which
I am thus
Undefended) of
Abidjan's ubiquitous
Transistors.

These the
Africans, as soon as
They – their barest first
Needs met – are able
To afford one,
Carry about with them
Nursed precariously
Upon the arm like
Babies: the aerial

Pulled out upward like
A sea-tossed
Ship's mast.

Through the black wall
You can just see,
Downwards, into a repair
Park for the
Cheap taxis that any

Ambitiously self-respecting
African takes

Always – and I
Do not: being more, both
Economical, and appreciative
Of the pleasures of
The landscape and
My legs.

Europeans of course
In general have
No legs. They roll
Always upon
Wheels of some
Sort, as if they were
Magicians, or of
A different
Species: in taxis

Or private cars, preferably
Expensive (never in the
Town's trim
Buses – or the small
Free-enterprise
Disintegrating lorries, with
A bench on each side
Inside, which ply
Everywhere like welcome and
Efficient midges), or on

New
Powered bicycles – which the
Africans buy
Too, once they've got
Their magical
Transistors.

The Europeans' is
A different
World – like a
Skyscraper
High above Africa. Africa's

Taxi-taking, bicycle and
Transistor classes
Make the sort of
Attempt to reach it
That a child makes, through
Its toys, to reach
The adult world. An attempt

Which has got at
Present about two
Perilous storeys
High: to about the
Level at which I
Am now
Sitting – a couple of
Storeys up – having

Breakfast, in luxury
Enough it
Seems to me (it is a
Mixed hotel
Of Africans and roughish
Europeans), between

The two worlds.

*

If I were living in a
Mud and grass
Hut across
The lagoon, looking out

At the new
Skyscraper of the Hôtel
Ivoire, where
Arriving Europeans
Lodge – as expensive as a
First class hotel in
Europe, and as ostentatiously
Pretentious as any
To be found there – what

Should I feel
About that symbol
Of us, that heaven
Which we hold

Out – high up, at
A distance, hardly
Attainable – that loud
Shop window
Showing what our
Culture, our intelligence
And history, have
To offer?

Awe?
Some Africans
Feel that. (You see

Them wandering past the hotel's
Swimming pool and
Bowling alleys, its
Bars, billiard tables and
Shut boutiques, in the evening, as though
They had been translated
Into the princess's castle in a
Fairy tale, and hoped one
Day to live
Always in some such
Bright world.) Or

A contemptuous, annihilating
Anger? Anger against

Power: against its
Emptiness – and
Its miserly
Clutching to itself of
What, to others, might
Be truly
Treasure. A destroying
And self-destructive
Anger. I'd

Choose anger. And
What I do feel
In fact is

Anger: against,
Not man's greed
Merely – that's almost
Corrigible, and at least has
Gusto – but his
Blindness: the lack
Of imagination that can
Create two
Such mutually
Unimaginable worlds, one
Emptily
Above the other. That

Is the dangerous
Sin: smallness,
Inability to see
The implications of the
Way in which we
Live. To
Grasp the scale of
Our, of all,
Existence. And

This we
All
Commit: both

The man in
That carpeted and air conditioned,
Servant ridden, inefficient
Skyscraper, and he across the

Loveliness of the lagoon
In his grass hut – who sleeps
On the earth floor,
Eventually, when the
Rest of his

Complicated family, of all
Ages, has stopped
Stepping over him
Among the cockroaches
In the heat and
Lies down on
It too.

*

However, I am neither
In the Hôtel
Ivoire (I was,
Though, lodged there
On my first
Night) nor
In a hut.

I am, today, on the
Balcony of this
Very different
Hotel, looking down
Past a glass of

Half drunk coffee and
A stripped off
Banana skin at
What can be seen
Of the courtyard
From this
Corner of it: two

Young palms, not
Very tall
Yet, coconuts bubbling
From the centre of their
Wealth of waving
Fronds (each
Frond-plume
Combed carefully, and
Parted); a flamboyant

Tree, the small light green
Acacia-like precisions of

Its large leaves
Flowerless, beneath the
Grey continually sunless
Sky; and over against
The far wall a
Few

Hibiscus bushes, the flower
Spitting out that long
Hibiscus style from
Its open, pressed back
Petals, like a bright
Figure of the act of love.

Among the flamboyant's
Horizontal planes of
Branches, and
The loose dry
Palm fronds (an unlikely
Enough place for
Perching), move
Small birds: much
Like sparrows but
Smaller, slimmer – the head a
Bluish grey and
The front
Greyish, ginger-brown upon the
Wings and back.

Beyond, just seen, are
The house tops – one storey
For the most
Part – of
Treichville, the
African part of this

Lagoon divided
Town: which till
Recently
Was held together
But by a
Single bridge.

2

The night's
Behind me – barely (as
I got up
Sunrise flooded
White light
Into the room). And

The day's work
Starts soon: not
To end
Till toward
Sunset – with a

Three hour break for
The siesta (which
I must
Fill in
Somehow – at my quiet desk
In the deserted office, or
Strolling about the
Centre of
The town) in the middle

Of the day when,
If the muffling
Cloud ceiling
Clears, or thins, the sun
Immediately above us
Raises the thermometer
From a steady
Humid eighty to the
Nineties: thirty
Degrees centigrade I
Should say.

The night
Is past. Before lies
All the zest
Of day: twelve hours
Of risen

Sun – thirteen or
So of
Daylight! This neat

Parcel of a day (here,
Near the equator,
Virtually the
Same size at
Any time of year) is laid
Each day
Before me: a new

Block of day, this
Mushroom town
In the grey-white
Light, and
The coast
Of Africa. Wealth,

Freedom! These
Lie out before
Me: lay
Out before me just
Now as I
Stepped onto the
Veranda, on
The first

Morning of the world.

Appetite! And
Not just for a
Breakfast of two
Bananas and a glass of coffee.

I sip the day, high
Up, above the private
Courtyard, and prepare –
At brief
Luxurious leisure – to
Launch out into
It: exposed, small

As the male
Member lost
In the act of love.

The smell of
Air, of the
Opening
Of things – of sky, out beyond
This courtyard
Anteroom, of sandy town
Streets and Africans, lagoon
Water, sea, and equatorial

Pressing forest
Dense as the damp
Cloud ceiling of
The sky above! Of a wide

World
Unknown – yet there
For you for the
Touching (stretch out
Your hand, walk
Out and
Down the street) – like

The body of a
Lover in the bed . . .

Would that my love
Were here: and that

This – unnecessarily,
Injuriously large beneath
The mosquito net – were
Our bed.

*

The block of
Night's
Behind me – of nighttime
Withdrawal into my
Inward
Self: into that which

I have been,
Within me, since
I was a
Child, since before
My birth, since –
Ever since since
Was. A black

Block which
I enter, each
Time as night
Recurs, through the
Cube – first – of
The shut
Lit room. In

That I write
Letters, loosen the
Tensions that have
Built up
Through the
Tautening
Day, look out
On the dark

Beyond us – deeper than that
Dark above of
Unexplored, disorientating
And yet
Authoritative stars – and eat

My bits of
Evening meal: idly
Flipping at mosquitos
With my handkerchief as they
Fly into this

Undefended fortress
Through the wall, so that
I may not be
Devoured when, soon, I'm
Stripped for that
Evening epicurean
Absolution, the

Cold shower – which makes
My entire body one
Clear
Palate, washed clean
Of the dead leaves of
The lived through day.

Inside the room's small
Cube, looms the
Core (a cone) of
The mosquito
Net: held up
From the ceiling by a
Ring, French
Fashion, from which
It falls like
A bridal veil – to be
Tucked in
Beneath the
Rectangle of mattress.

Entering this
Next, I – inside it –
Read a while: sneering
At the mosquitos which
Perch, glaring at me
Through the mesh (a mean
Schoolboy's pleasure
It is to
Cheat them; but they
Go too far). Sleep.
Dream . . .

And a little of what
I dream – as if of
Another life – is, next

Day, fleetingly
Remembered: scraps
Which change, in part, their
Outline and their meaning as
They precipitate on
Conscious
Recollection – as unknown
And interesting a world
As any
Africa. I spend

Half of these
Breakfast minutes now
Walking out through
Those dreams'
Thinning fringe: through, not
Their forms
So much, as the
Experienced
Substance of what
Was
In sleep.

*

Awake – quite awake
By now, and sharply
Present in
This place (which
I know just enough to be
Aware, with a wide
Adventurous pleasure, of how
Little of it, alive
There before me, I
Do know) – I shut and

Lock, for one more
Day, the
Door; unroll
The staircase; shake
Hands with the
Room
Boy (who lives out

Beyond Port Bouet – where
His new born baby
In this African
Winter weather, dangerously,
Has a cold), using the few
Well worn words of
French that are
Currency between us
Once again to
Convey a mutual
Warmth, a recognition of
What we have in
Common – the simple
Human state – which is

About as much as
One can
Convey to
Anyone; cross, down

Below, the
Courtyard (the ground
Is damp: there's been
A powdering
Of rain), and walk

Free into this new
Immense morning, out
Into the street.

Half an hour's
Hard walking then across
Treichville – the entirely
African, poor
Section
Of the town – and the

Bridge (some half
Mile long), to
The 'Plateau': where are
Abidjan's commercial and

Administrative buildings – small
Skyscrapers – the morning

Market and
My office. A

Wholly
African office: staffed
By bewildered people
From all
The states of Africa, and
By us few

Spare parts, the European
Linguists – French and English –
Who they need
At conference times, alas
For them, if they are to

Converse with one another.

II

THROUGH TREICHVILLE TO THE BRIDGE

1

In each day in
The morning: back again at
Dusk. And on the

Way this half
Hour's walk
Through
Africa. Or through
The part of it

On lagoon
Promontories and islands
Which is this
Prosperous town, sprung up
Like a mushroom: the
Port of half
The ex-French West African
States and their manufacturer
Of light industrial goods; full

Of young people – and small children –
Half of them from
The other African
Countries round, come
In to find
Employment, high wages and the
Magic of our
Paradisal West.

*

'Take us,' the young boys
Say (inland in
The Ivory Coast), clinging
To your car, 'take us
With you to
Abidjan!' – as one
Might say, to
Heaven. Aspiration,
Hope, the way

Ahead –
Lie here.

So too
In the night clubs
Of Treichville, which the local
French – and
Visiting Europeans of
All sorts, and
Sailors from the port – frequent, the
Girls, charming, charmingly
Dressed, and beautiful like so
Many of these
People, offer themselves,
Open and easy, amateur, to
Share – not just
The money – but the
Radiance, the brilliance,
That shines
Out from
The magic West.

For the West is
Magical. These transistors, concrete
Buildings, the bright cotton
Cloths of the
Dresses in the streets, oil for
People's lanterns, tins
Of milk – ships, aeroplanes – and
The town's mechanics, senior
Officials, managers, small
Industrialists, all

Materialize out of the
Blank
Sea and sky from
The unseen, unbelievable, in
Everything to be
Emulated
West. One aspires
Here to live a

Life which is
Not of

This place: and lives
Therefore – trailing
Behind – by the
Courtesy
Of France: with which one
Never can
Catch up.

From this admiration
It is easy
To progress to
Envy and
A bitter hate. The more bitter
Because what
Binds, what enslaves
One, is
Not only
Colonists, or Europeans
Even, but

Oneself: one's own
Desires' contradictions
In the position
One's been born
In. The West

Has won; and the world
Moves in its wake.

Has won – at the
Moment. For already
The picture
Complicates: is reshaping
Itself. Nothing in life

Moves in a
Straight line. What seems
Certain, inescapable,
Today – looks quite
Different tomorrow. Every
Day it's
A new morning.

So
Don't despair. Or feel
Secure either. All things
Bend.

At any rate it's
Good to see
That since I was here
For a few
Days
Six years
Back, there have been –
Thanks to
Independence – certain
Startling changes. Not

Merely (an ambiguous
Benefit) in
The look of the town – many
More new
Buildings, and a second
Landscape-long straight
Bridge – but

In the bearing
Of the people. They
Do not, as they did
Then, glance aside
And wait until you
Speak – but look
You level
In the eye, like free
Men, like people; and often
Call out to me
A greeting: 'Ça va?', 'Bon jour!',
'Bon jour, Monsieur!' Or
More frequently – at any
Time of day – 'Bon
Soir!' Or

'Bon soir, Papa!' In Africa
It's honour to
Be Dad.

So Independence is
Independence
After all – to an
Extent. And if
Africa is not
Independent of
Our wealth, our power, our
Glamour – neither

Are we, God
Help us. We're
Caught, enslaved
By the
Damn thing too.

There's only one
World
After all; and
You can't get
Out of it. Nobody can.
The whole creation's
In it. There's
One ring round the

Lot: a circle.
The centre of
Which is
Me, or you –
Or one of
My mosquitos or a
Hibiscus bush – whatever
The individual door may be

One chances to have
Entered this
World by – and so
To look out from
At the rest.

*

Stiffened, solidified by
Breakfast, erect, awake, I

Step out
From the door into the
Wide
Morning (the ring
Of the horizon, round,
Like a woman
Round me) and stride

Out, as
A brisk swimmer
Strikes out, in a
Sea of
Zest – alight with
Interest every
Way I look.

Sand of the broad
Roadside; and a long
Ditch – full in
Places of
Stagnating water: which

No doubt
Accounts for my
Mosquitos. There are
Fewer of these they
Say in the densely
Built up
Crowded and so
Standing-water-less
Centre of
Treichville.

Treichville
Is laid out
In a neat
Grid of
Avenues and
Small
Side streets: with trees
To lead the eye on
Into, and

Sometimes close,
The vista – and,

When the sun
Is hot, to give
Shade for one to
Sit in, or to lie
Out in in the
Siesta (unless
Then you
Choose your

House's dark, bare swept
Interior – or the sharp
Shade of a wall). The

Trees are, mostly, of
That species which when young
Shoots up
Ridiculously from flat
Tier to again flat
Horizontal tier, and has
Thick dark-green large
Leaves which
Bud (and,
Dead, drop)
Red.

Despite the grid, or
Because of it, this is a
Perfect place for
Getting
Lost in. The main
Approach roads strike
Across the chessboard
At a shallow
Angle, which you never
Entirely accurately
Allow for – so that

Imagining you have
Worked out right
The plus and minus sum
Of your stroll's

Quite
Simple angles, you
Find yourself

Coming from
The opposite direction toward the
Point you
Started from; and
Have to
Begin again; and
Again. Unless
You're lucky. Rectangular

Reason, inflexible,
Defeats itself; rigid, is
Irrationality. For life
Is not like
That: not
The slow
History
That creates
A place, nor – here – the

Larger logic of
The landscape from which the
Traffic comes and,
Surrounding the stiff
Grid on
All sides,
The shores of the lagoon.

One feels one's
Going mad: that there
Is no
Right answer.

However, the avenues
Are wide, and
Paved; and the side

Streets – half
Metalled, half of sand (with
Ephemeral puddles, that dry
Up quick

Enough) – are broad
For separating
Houses of
One storey (indeed, one
Room), however
Full of
People and frothing
With small children: people who
Cook, and wash, and sit, and trade, and
Machine up clothes for
Sale, all out on
The street side.

*

The oblique main
Motor road
Outside my hotel takes
Me – with one half
Turn (and
Mind that you don't
Miss it) – to

The bridge.

Down the middle
Of it runs a
Narrow
Footpath island – from which
A row of trees spreads
Shade, umbrella fashion, right
From one side of the
Twin roadway
To the other: roofing it.
The lower
Branches of the

Trees, before they
Droop too
Low, are cut
Unskilfully down with
Murderous
Blunt instruments – reduced
To hacked-about long

Raw splintered
Stumps. No need is felt

To be considerate to
Plants, here
Where each twig
Thrust into the moist
Soil leaps
Generously
To life – and
No sooner is the
Gardener's back
Turned than equatorial
Forest, dense and lush, springs
Up again on
All sides, tall,
From this sandy
Flat
Lagoon land.

I walk along
The central
Island, stepping over tree
Roots – and aside to
Let pass young men
Coming from the
Opposite direction: or women,

Their market basket on
Their head, and
A baby, a year or two
Old it may be, held
On the hip and feeding –
As the mother
Walks on
With the other
Women – at the
Large lax
Breast (which it

Can reach
Round to
And lift up
For itself
Till it has that

Casual constant
Plaything, that key
Joy of its infant
Empire, the
All-its-life-long familiar
Nipple
In its mouth).

An older woman,
Carrying a bucket
Of clothes, for washing, on
Her head – with a baby
On her back and two scattering
Small children
To herd – breaks
From the island's kerb and
Makes a dash
Across the road in a
Lull in
The traffic, with ungainly

Caution holding the
Level basket
Balanced
While the sleeping baby
Bounces, heavy and loose,
Against her from
Behind: her eyes,
Wary and scared – with
Reason – watching
At once the arbitrary
Cars (which she was
Not brought
Up with) in the
Distance, and
Her chickens.

I too
Cross. I must turn
Off here,
From the oblique
Motor road, onto
One of the
Grid's straight
Side streets.

2

Behind the first row
Of houses in this
Side
Street, here where the
Town grows
Dense – its early morning

Privacies displayed,
African fashion, out in
The open street – the

Mother, with her
Brood diminutive
About her, joins
The bright many
Coloured crowd
At an open-sided
Shelter, where are the
Public taps and
Wash troughs. There women
And small girls are
Doing their washing; or

Waiting to fill up
Buckets and basins – not
Pots in
This town (a large flat
Basin, almost full, moves
Off at about
The height of
My elbow on
A small girl's
Head) – to take

Down narrow streets, along
Roads, through the
Traffic, home.

The women stand
Straight legged – their
Behinds square

In the air: hands in the
Full wash-bucket
On the floor.

One cloth – of bright
Red, gold, green or
Yellow
Cotton, printed (in
France perhaps
Or Holland) with
Brilliant fantasies
Based upon still
For the most part
Identifiable
Indigenous designs – is
Wrapped round the
Hips, down almost
To the floor. Another

Of the same stuff
Is loosely wrapped
About the torso. (Many women
Here in the town, richer
Than these, wear
Also a

Bodice; and wind this
Second cloth, instead,
Provocatively round
The haunches, or wherever –
Higher – elegance,
Fancy or the
Heat
Suggests.) Within

This the long
Breasts, heavy and
Loose, or empty
Flat, hang
Forward,
Down: helpless –
Sympathetically in the
Same direction
As the woman's working

Arms and
Head – a fruit

Exotic, equatorial,
African, full of
Desire's treasure and
Of children's
Comfort, to greet
The grateful eye
Each day upon the
Tree of morning. While

Yet a third
Cloth attaches the
Baby: its head now
Downward – down
The bending
Mother's back.

*

Babies
Not only sleep
Upon the mother's
Back while she does
Her vigorous
Washing – but also

As, spruce and neat,
With something of
Superior disdain, she
Sails past on her powered
Bicycle; or walks

Stately to market, basket
Tall upon her
Head; or bargains
At her stall.

To tie on her
Baby – which may be
Of any age up to
Two or so (and may
Wear a bright

Knitted woollen
Bonnet, to keep
Off the
Sun) – the mother,

Standing, bends at
Rightangles, the baby
Forward, flat, upon
Her horizontal
Back; spreads over him
The cloth; ties the
Lower edge of it
(Tucked in beneath his
Buttocks) firmly round
Her waist; and,
Straightening, secures
The top edge (tucked in
Beneath itself and held
By its own
Tightness) flattening
Across the
Springing of her breasts
Where it takes
The best
Part of his weight: as
If he were
In a sack. Only

His head's
Left out – and
As he grows
Older, his

Feet. These
Are thrust out
Forward – so that
As she comes toward
You the woman seems
To have, not a
Baby (it is concealed
Behind her), but
An extra pair of
Infant feet

Of her own, at
Waist level: asking, as

Children's feet do,
To be
Taken in your hand.

When the sun is
Strong a further,
Fourth light cloth
May be thrown
Over the mother's
Shoulders and the
Baby's head, covering
The child
Completely, so that
It's just a
Swathed low
Hump: a kind of
Pregnancy long past
Its time, behind.
And once I saw

A woman – walking
In a light
Wind – let this cloth
Float out
In the air, from her
Half raised hands, behind
Her, so that it made a
Gay airy
Awning for her baby against
The assault of the high
Sun, unsheathed
In the bare sky.

*

When it needs to
Be fed
The baby – once old
Enough to
Straddle – is slung
Round to the hip, and
Held there with

One arm: as a young
Child of our own
Is sometimes
Carried. Beyond the age
At which we
Suckle ours, it takes up
For itself, with its

Small hands, the breast's loose
Treasure
Negligently (never
Avid, since not left
Long enough
In need) and lifts
It up – its
Plaything since the day that
It was born – till it can
Nuzzle at
The nipple (looking round,
Up, at you),
While the mother

Strides on, with her
Other burdens, briskly
Homeward or
About her business, talking to
Her friends. A better

Sight this than our
Own children, walking
With a plastic feeding
Bottle hanging
From the teeth, or
Plugged up with a
Comforter. And
It is better no
Doubt too
For the child; though

Worse for
The mother's ravaged
Breast: the sight of
Which – ruined, flattened,
Hanging – disspirits

Me, egotist that I
Am: an adult
Desiring male
Ever ready on the
Draw, dizzily
Upon the brink
Of mating.

3

Just here, where the
Pavement widens –

And drying clothes are
Hung on the fence that
Separates off
The roadway and

Spread out
Flat upon the ground to
Finish drying (too dry
Already, though you
Might not think it,
To pick
Up the red
Dust) beside the
Feet of
Passers by – is

A bench, in
The contemplative
Shade of a few
Gum trees, round which a
Squad of children
Usually are
Playing: at the age

When they have left
Their mother's back and adventure
Out, in small droves, away
From her – though
Not very far, still
Within crying
Out and
Calling distance: just round the
Corner from her door. Black

Of course, as
Everybody

Else is – except my startling
Self – lively, lovely
Many of them, entirely
Enchanting. One,

One day, a boy of
About three, in a shift to
Just below the
Waist, advanced – as I
Passed by
As usual – stoutly toward
Me with
A hand held up and
Out, to
Be shaken. 'Ça va?' – the

Adult greeting . . .

Children quite often do
That – in the town, and
In those African
Outlying far flung-out
Suburbs to
Which one
Needs to take a bus.

Parents if they are
There (a father –
Work finished, in
The evening, squatting on his
Doorstep in the dusk,
Another child
Between his knees – or a
Mother, entirely without
French as
Most of the women
Are, camped quietly
On the sociable
Ground at some
Busier street's
Kerbside, selling her
Few oranges, or eggs, or groups
Of three bananas) then
Also give

A greeting,
Smiling; a bridge thus
Made, adult and
Intimate, between us –
At a level at which,
Whether or
Not we have a
Common language, and despite
The difference of history
And circumstance between
Us, we understand
Each other
Perfectly. The exchange
Is, not
Only to me I
Think, a
Peculiarly refreshing
Envigorating pleasure.

The smile
Becomes an outright
Broad laugh of amused
Indulgence and
Complicity when

Children – round a
Mother squatting in
The evening on the
Ground before her door – suddenly
Like a shying flock take
Fright, at
The sight of the
Passing
European (seeing his
Alien eye
Upon them) and seek
Shelter
Behind her.

This gay amusement
Of the women shows
That they must

Feel, as I
Do, relief
At the abrupt removal
Of the barricades raised,
Invisible, bewildering,
Between our two
Worlds – and the
Discovery, fleeting
But brilliant like
The flash of a wing, of
Common, level, human ground
Between us.

Children are, thank
God, children . . .

*

Not that invariably
One likes their
Being children. Just as

At home, in wartime, our
Children
Begged from the
Over rich and over
Generous Americans, so here
At times a
Child (and not
A poor one, which would
Be different
Entirely) hovers about
One, like a midge: 'Monsieur,
Tu me donnes
Dix francs. Dix francs,
Monsieur!' 'If I

'Were your Dad I'd
Skin you.' They get an
Old fashioned lecture: well
Brought up children do
Not ask
For money. No doubt

They do not
Understand me, except perhaps
The tone. Those cadging words
May be, almost, all the
French
They know. However,

You must act as is
Natural to
You – and, speaking
As you are
Able, observe your
Own conventions; then something
Perhaps may
Get across. If
You don't
Nothing can.

The first thing,
If you want
To communicate, is
To be
Yourself – whatever
That is. Do not act
As you imagine may
Make sense to
Other people: do not
Try to
Share their language of
Behaviour, especially
If it is very
Foreign, very strange,
To you. Thus I

Find myself saying
'Monsieur' and 'Madame', and
'Vous', to
Everyone – unusual
Though those
Courtesies may be –
Whatever tongue,
French or African, I am
Addressed

In; and even when
The other (as the custom
Is – acquired from the
French, who spoke
With a European
Familiar lack
Of respect to
Africans) says, if
He speaks French,
'Tu'. Be

Yourself. And
See
The other
Person: there,
Like yourself, before
You. Although in

Africa – as
Everywhere else, God
Knows – each
Goes about
Clad in the heavy
Armour
Of his own
Distant distinct
World, barbarously
Disguised.

*

I shake the
Small boy's
Hand. 'Ça va?' And at once

A crowd of hands are
Held out, up, to
Me, round me, to be
Shaken: half a
Dozen – more. Children of
All ages, up to
Nine or ten. In
The bag over my

Shoulder (with lunch
In it, and writing
Paper) is a tin of
Soap solution,
And a stick with a
Ring at the end, for
Blowing bubbles. Sitting

On the bench, I
Extract
It: slowly, with
Difficulty – one's
Bag gets
In a muddle, and I am not
Sure at first that
Today I
Have this with
Me. (Being now

A grandfather, usually
I have – that
Or balloons, or
Something; one needs
Them: leaping at the
Chance to
Be – two
Generations later, without
Selfconsciousness – a small
Child again.) A silence

Of solidifying, intensifying
Anticipation. They pile up
Round me – on
Me – on
The bench. At last I

Have it
Out. Incomprehension. I raise
The stick:
Blow gently.
Nothing happens. Again: a few
Bubbles – they float off,

Many coloured, light
Upon the air, among the
Surrounding faces.
Admiration! And
Apprehension; soon allayed.
More. The bubbles
Drift away, high – down
The street, round the
Corner of a house. I have all
My audience's
Attention: they cry out
Like the crowd at
A football match when
Someone scores a goal. Low
Bubbles are caught
Quick – as if by
Pouncing kittens. There are

Now about twenty
Children. I feel as
Though I were in the
Middle of
A black

Ant-heap. Climbing
Out, I move round
Behind the back
Of the bench: the
Children line
Up, on
It – and here at my
Side
Of it surge
About my knees.
One go

For you – starting
With the youngest (who
Is slow) – and you, and
You; then back
To the first again. They
Can all
Do it. Even that
Boy of twelve

Who is
Slightly simple.

The feel of those
Young puppy
Bodies all
Over me is entirely
Delightful. Delicious. And

Their absorbtion in
What is going
On: in the

Exhaustless
Birth and release of
Those magical, irridescent,
Ephemeral, freely
Floating bubbles, almost
Weightless, sensitive
To the finest invisible
Thread of motion
In the air.

We too have, and
Enjoy together,
Common ground: for
Which I
Am grateful.

Now I
Must get on
To work. I
Extricate myself. And a changing

Wind of interest
Scatters them once again, almost
Before I've gone.

*

One day, I saw
Some of those
Same children
Playing a game

Equally absorbing: beating
(These were all
Boys) with sticks
At something
Hung up on a fence. It
Was a dying
Lizard. And

Another day
In a street in the town
I passed a gay
Gang, chanting
A song as they
Marched along
In a procession. Before
Them, on two sticks,
Hobbled a
Mocked
Cripple – their
Own age.

Children
Are children. And will
Be men, women – little
Altered. Angel

And devil. So we
All are. Here
In miniature
In children is
Our adult
World: the same
World the
World over.

Yet how delightful
The feel of those
Unselfconscious
Puppy bodies
Crawling, confidingly, all
Over me, submerging
Me like a sea – the boys'

Cropped
Heads' harsh

Lamb's wool, and the
Girls' hair
Teased out into
Tufts from a scalp
Mapped out like
A chessboard, one
Tuft to each
Square!

Born, we are
Thrown naked
Among loves and
Lions. Hyenas!

4

At the next corner beyond
The bench a
Young man
Squats: abstracted, half in
Meditation – wearing a white
Long shift, which covers him
Completely, and a small fez
Scullcap – a bowl before him,
Empty. He is there

In the roadside
Dust
Each day.
Mohammedans give

Alms. And little
Enough is needed to
Buy a man
His food (except
At the Hôtel Ivoire,
Where you pay for one meal
Enough to cater for
An army). Occasionally a
Few francs
Are dropped
In. Time

Does not have
Importance, is an edgeless
Ocean in
Which existence
Is, not an anxious
Thing that's
Measured on a ruler: for him

The world, till the pain of his
Existence comes to be
Too much, stands
Still. With one

Hand he holds
His beads; and beside the

Bowl, before
Him, lies a small
Pile of
Cowrie shells.

Beggars however
Are relatively
Rare. Except
Cripples in
The wealthy
Centre of the town. They

Do not do so
Badly. One,
Both legs deformed and
Paralyzed, hails
One day – as I am
Sitting in it – a
Free-plying passing
Bus; and is hauled up
Onto the high hard
Tailboard. Whereupon he
Pays the usual fare
Out to the suburb that he
Sleeps in. Being

Three feet
Shorter than the rest
Of us, hopping on his
Hands along the ground, does not
Seem to
Disconcert him; he is used
To being as
He is – as we
Are to being
Leggèd. And sitting on the
Bench inside the bus
We all, the same
Height now, look – as
We are –
Equal. Including

An old lady, hardly
Clad at all and a

Little dotty, who offers me
A piece of her half
Coconut: which she is scooping
Out, appreciatively, with a
Bit of broken shell.

*

From the oblique broad
Motor road that
I first set
Out on strike
Avenues – crossed by
Smaller sandy
Side streets, like
The one I next turned
Into – into the

Thick
Of Treichville

Along one of these,
At a corner, is
The shop
Where I buy
Most of
My provisions: open all
Day, and
Half the night.
Upon the doorstep

Sits a woman, with
Small pyramids of
Limes, a few
Bananas and a
Pair perhaps of
Paw-paws, set out for
Sale beside her: a child
At her knee, and another, half
Asleep, toying with her
Wide breast.

The shop
Itself is a
Minute

Cube, solid with
Wares – tiny
Tins of milk, packets of
Soap powder, lanterns, eggs,
Bottles of beer,
Baskets, almost
Anything you could want – into
The middle of which has
Been inserted
Somehow a
Large drum of
Paraffin; also
A counter,
Waist height. Behind that
Is usually –

On the floor – the
Owner's wife, with their
Small children; and always
The proprietor
Himself: standing, talking to
Friends who casually drop
In, and briskly
Serving customers.

Shut, the shop
Becomes no doubt
Their home: though
There is hardly enough
Clear floor
Space for a
Body to
Lie down on. The woman

On the step (whose goods
Are sold for her
By the proprietor
When she is
Away a moment) then goes
Back to her own
Home, in some
Obscurer alley.

*

Food in the open, at
The street side (fruit, fish
Grilling in the evening over
Braziers, and coarse plantains
And corn cobs roasted
Upon embers), is
Sold by
Women
Only: who camp
Out, there among the
Passing feet,
Calmly and sociably – all
Day it may be –
With their children.

While clothes, shoes
And European
Oddments – overflowing
The pavements in the busier
Avenues – are sold
Exclusively by
Men. And men

Are the
Clothes makers.
In the side alleys
At the centre of
Treichville, by
The mosque, these
Sit at their
Sewing machines
Under a
Rough shelter – or
In shacks, elbow to
Elbow at their tables,
Almost in
The dark – machining up

Long shift-shaped
Cotton robes in

Various plain
Colours (dull green or
Yellow, white,
Harsh blue) embroidered
More or less
Elaborately, Mohammedan
Style, at the
Neck: which,
Finished, are

Displayed – hung up – outside
The shack door, or from the
Shelter's roof, on coat
Hangers consisting
Of one
Stick, like
The crosspiece of a scarecrow:
So that they look
Like a bedsheet
Airing. Others make

Men's jerkins, with a
Round neck, slit and
Machine-embroidered down
The front, of printed
Cotton: in every colour,
And of every kind of
African-inspired harsh
Impetuous
Design; and even with
Gentle floral
European patterns such as
Might, with us, be
Worn by small
Girls, or
Old ladies.

The robes, put
On, fall
From the shoulders to the
Feet (their pockets – one
Each side, inside, at
The breast – often, too
Full, sagging

Down, destroying the
Clear straight
Garment's shape): cut
Narrow, with the sleeves
Right from
The armpit, or

Enveloping the webbed
Man entirely
Like a cloud (sleeves
Little more than
Hand holes, from the
Wrist), wide
As both arms
Outstretched. They fall

With a Mohammedan plain
Dignity – magnifying
The wearer to a
Single enlarged
Statement, like a god – or

Anyhow, untidily, as
Though they were
The wrong size
And slipping off.

The jerkins, with their
Pagan African
Designs, are almost
Shirt size: and worn
Dashingly – or in
Tatters, washed so
Often that the
Stuff has
Split – with
Trousers.

Odd ends of
Material are
Machined up
Into thigh-length

Shifts – a patchwork
Of irregular
Long narrow strips –
For the bare-leg'd
Heavy labourers.

*

The mosque,
Among the crowds and cars and
Commerce (everyone in

Abidjan seems
To live by
Selling things
To someone else), presents

Cool areas
Of greyish white
Outside, mounting to
Four low
Minarets – and is
A high, great, dim
Cave of

Peace
Within. Prayer mats
And emptiness. Beside

It, encamped upon the
Pavement, are
Elderly men – the trimmed
White beard
Startling
Against the brown-black
Face – each with
His mat and
Water kettle, the rest of
His possessions being
Hung up, as though he
Meant to live there for
Some time, on
The mosque's
Outer wall. Beads

In hand, they have
Small piles of cowrie
Shells before them, and
Perhaps a few white
Skull caps
To sell. Some –

Stretched right out –
Sleep, beneath the
Legs of
The passers by: painfully,
With the dignified uncomfortable
Pathos of the aged.

In this
New town, these
Are almost the only
Old people
That you
See: the past

And the outdated
Wisdom – the solidity,
Weight, worth – of the
Old
Of Africa are

Elsewhere: inland, where
Indigence, hunger,
Hardships
Are, and memory's
Long root – in
Those vast
Tracts, horizon

Beyond horizon and
Horizon
And horizon, of
Yet
Unaltered land.

5

I cross the last
Of the parallel
Street-intersecting
Avenues. Houses

Are gone – and
Before me a
Bare slope
Stretches (where in
The evening young
Men play
Barefoot
Football) at the

Far edge of
Which small
Ferry boats
Are filling up
With passengers, and their
Bundles: to cross to

Various points in
The mosaic
Of the lagoon.

Above
Sails the bridge: straight out,
Half a mile
Across grey
Water, beneath the
Still-grey sky – from which

Through a thinning of
The clouds may
Strike down
Sheets of
Diffuse sunlight,
That shake out
In joy the wide
Water revelation

Of the warm
Fresh day.

High up, I
Walk across – full
Of the morning's
Vigour, and just
Fast enough
Almost
Not to sweat.

*

Far on each
Side are low
Lagoon
Shores, densely grown with
Bright green
Vegetation and the
Darker irregularity of
Great trees (on

A ridge, one
Stands tall above all
Others like a
Monument, against
The morning), seen

Across the water's
Ripples, which catch
Silver light: upon whose

Immense space the slip
Of a
Dugout canoe, here and there,
Paddles with
Its small cargo.

Every day, every
Moment, the live
Surface of this
Water
Alters. And at

Night as
I walk back
Home the sky – and
The sheet of water
Lifted up
Beneath it, holding
Its spilt last
Brightness – turn

Lavender,
Then violet; while

In the altering light
The yellow-red of
Sunset riots low
Down, out
Beyond the far shore
To my right, where
Is the

Ocean.

Exaltation: between
Land and land,
Water and the sky!

The shores are, everywhere,
Mossed with
Vegetable life. And
Behind me
Now in
Treichville, and before
On the Plateau, rise
Solid shapes of
White light
Buildings just emerging – like
Something you have
Half thought
Of – through

That moss, that fur, of
Green.

*

I pick my way past
Puddles, and people
Walking at various
Slower speeds
In front: zigzagging
To avoid knots of people
Coming to meet me
Head on the
Other way. All

Men: in that
Straight
Long robe, or short
Brisk tunic; or (for

Among the many
Africans from other
States are, also,
Ghanaians – Ghana is not
Far off) a
Toga: wrapped about
The body
To the bare
Knee, and thrown
Over one black
Naked
Shoulder. An immense
Man thus toga'd

Walks
Like a prince, an
Archangel: slowly,
Serene, with a calm wide
Magnificent
Assurance; unselfconscious,
Entirely at

His ease. A great
Broad Ghanaian face. Life

Makes space
Around him. He is
A mountain, among the
Beauty of the day.

And others of these
Young faces that I
Pass – and some,
More anxious,
Older – have
A clear, dark
Decisive beauty
That makes, later, the
Features of my European
Colleagues look
Insipid, incohesive, like
Inconsistent jottings made on
Pallid paper: till one's eye

Becomes used to their white
Idiom again.

I must admit though
That I find young
Africans, men or
Women, hard
To tell from
One another (those smooth
Pleasantly proportioned
Features in
The black) and
At times get them
Confused. So I hardly

Can complain when
Africans, at the office, confuse
Me with another
Englishman I do not
Particularly like – half
A head shorter – who also
Wears a beard. Any bearded

White man is the
Same man: we two
Present one easily
Distinguishable feature
In the blinding general
Blank whiteness, that
Makes us all
Look as alike as sheep.

*

The bridge
Ends: dips
Down
Into the rising
Streets, and quite
Different town
Tempo, of the

Plateau.

The lagoon's
Behind me. The day with
Its office work extends
Before: till,

Violet and orange,
Darkening, its
Flower
Closes, across the
Lagoon water, as
I return

To Treichville. That – with
Its black
Faces, and families
Living in one and
Two room houses – has
Become, for this
Month or so, my
Home: the place

Which, in alien
Africa, I do
Not need, alert, to
Adjust myself
To; where
I am

Myself, unthinking,
Accepting and accepted; can
Sink into
The substance
Of things, within
Myself. And sleep.

III

ON THE PLATEAU

1

You'd think that they were
Fruit, those blackish
Untidy parcels hanging
From the tops of
The high trees –
Where the foliage thins a
Little – in

The middle of the town
Up on the
Plateau . . .

*

Here, from a central
Square with
Gardens – and
The bright life
Of the vegetable and
Fruit market – streets
And avenues, between
Mature shade-shedding
Trees, strike out
On all

Sides: flanked by
Sophisticated shops, and office blocks –
And, as the town
Loosens, Ministries, the Parliament
House, police headquarters,
Barracks and private

Villas set
Back among dusty
Gardens piled high
With tropical
Exuberant vegetation.

The Plateau
Is a promontory
Thrust out – raised

Up a little – into the
Lagoon. From it,

Every time the trees
And houses
Open to
Disclose the distance,
The lagoon again
Appears – and every way
You look the

Land bends
Down (as if you
Could, here, step off
The world's
Edge) – except in

One
Direction. There
Buses race out
Along straight roads
To an African
Outlying suburb,
Adjamé - a dense,
Dusty, lusty
Shack-world, in whose bareness
People take the
Place of vegetation: before

The green
Countryside
Opens out and,
Almost at once, the
Forest.

*

You go on thinking
They are fruit of
Some sort (that

Is, you do if
You are someone who
Looks up at
All, who looks
About him
A little, which few
Do: we

Chug on,
Shut into our
Carriage, along the railway
Line of what we have decided
Once and for all life
Is – in
Our own small
Cell – complaining that
Existence, our life as
We have made it
And insist with
Panic that it
Must remain, is
Small) until

You see
One
Move. The skin of
That particular
Lumpy hanging
Bundle, at one side,
Partly
Detaches itself
And shifts a
Little its
Position.

Hung up there on
The bare branch
Above the town, it is a
Cluster – dry,
Insectine – of

Bats: as
Closely packed
Together as
Brown smoked
Kippers, up
To a dozen
Of them; the great
Wings folded
And the feet
Hooked, all together,
On the branch
At the same
Point, like a
Fruit's stem.

The town is thus,
In the middle, a
Bat
Orchard. Hung
With hives
Of bats. Seeing

That one
Bundle slightly
Move, one feels
The place is
Infested, crawling
With an insectine
Aerial withdrawn
Life that may

Burst into
Its own at
Any moment. Almost,
One itches.

*

If these were
Fruit it would not
Be surprising. For,
To the ignorant

Temperate-zone
Stranger, Africa each
Day presents
New, magnificent, plant

Impossibilities: fruits,
Flowers, beyond his measured
Quiet conception, beyond
Imagination; trees
With bold unheard of
Hieroglyphics of leaf
Language – tall as a
Street is long, capacious
As a street for
Aerial
Habitation – their trunk
Some other earth's
Thick
Axis; and

Gargantuan-leaved, sepentine,
Oceanic swarming never
Ending creeper. You'll

See examples, there
Below the bats,
In the town's
Public gardens . . .

There dealers, from stalls
Beneath bright coloured
Canvas awnings,
Sell tourist
Junk of
All sorts, and some
Still quite
Interesting objects – carved
Wood, cast metal – which

Get steadily
More debased each
Year as they
Sink toward
The taste of the

Rich
White customers. Step

Near and
The dealer-flies are
At once
At you, thrusting
Into your hands
Preposterous objects
You'd pay to
Get away from, and – should
You pause before
Refusing, out of
Courtesy, or show
A glimmer of emergent
Interest in
Something else
Hidden in the heap –
Demanding five times the
Reasonable price (prepared

To bargain – with
The absorbed intent
Skill of a
Tightrope dancer – yet
Not to be
Beaten down too
Far: for you after
All are
Rich and they
Have to live) . . .

Here are grass
Lawns, where lizards
Run like ghostly
Flickering
Visions; rocklike
Cactuses; bushes of

Hibiscus (the flower,
Held out upon
The stem, large
As your face – as
Yourself it

Seems if you gaze
Into it – utterly
Devoid of
Reticence: the style's
Tongue all
Out, outspoken, thrust out
From the pressed
Back petals which, light
On the air, are generous
As a woman wholly
Given, nothing
Of herself
Withheld). Among

These grows a
Low tree, from
Whose bark
Swell out – suddenly one
Day I am
Aware of it – light

Green smooth
Balloons, as big as
Footballs. Another small

Tree has, among leaves so
Large and
Deeply fretted that
They seem – rather than
Leaves – elegantly bold
Exotic
Banners, hanging

Green fruit the
Size of my
Two hands,
A-prickle
With a fur of
Small
Protuberances: very neat. What
Fruit will
That be? While all

Over the town are
Mangoes, bursting into

A yellowish down of
Flower among the
Lumped together dark
Willow-like masses of
Their leaves – whose
Fruit, gradually
Ripening as the weeks
Proceed, hangs

Reservedly straight
Down, like
A chrysalis, on a
String of stalk,
The amorphous shape of some
Internal organ: hoarding
Their wealth
Within.

No shape – no size – of
Fruit would be
Impossible. Trees stand
And casually offer what
Is outside all
Reason with which
We are
Familiar: beyond the
Bounds of any
Fantasy of which we
From the cool
North are
Capable. Here

It is. You
Can touch it. Make

Of it
What you can.

2

Sometimes, in broad daylight
In the middle
Of the day, during
The siesta, when Africans

Chat
Quietly or sleep
Stretched out on the
Public gardens'
Benches or the grass, when

Those dealers who
Have not gone home
Lie before, or
Beneath, the trestles
Of their stalls (half shut
Now, and covered
Over, left
Abandoned by
Life's tide) – while

The town
Empties, and porters
At the office
Sleep, sitting at
Their desks (which
Command the empty
Corridors
And the abruptly
Fallen silence
Of the stairs) – some

Unusual stirring
Of the traffic, or a
Boy perhaps
With his unkind
Catapult, will disturb

The hanging
Dormitory, half hidden
High up among the
Upper leaves, that

Orchardful of
Night-flying winged
Fruit; and one
Or two, then

Ten, two dozen, large bats
Will detach themselves
And plane low
Above the tree tops, like
A flight of rooks. But
Look at
Them – against the
Light – and you
See not
Feathers, but a boned
Half-transparent
Membrane of
Planing
Slowly rowing
Wing: with, before,

A large
Mouse head, furred,
Intelligent, the size
Of a stout
Rat's. The air is

Full of
Skittering, not a
Squeak, quite,
Or twitter – a restless
Dry sound, sharp, from
All sides, part exclamation
And part
Conversation, not as loud
As, but continuous like,
The sound of
Starlings – as those
Great sheets of

Dark wing (a light
Soft honey-colour
Beneath) fly up
From the leaves, plane

Round, and then (still
Half asleep
No doubt, as one
Is when
One gets up
In the night) settle

Back among the
Others,
Hanging from a branch
Bare against
The sky's
Light, or
Beneath the high
Surface
Of the leaves. As

Those that
Peeled off
Come back, the
Hanging bundle
Stirs, and each part
Of it (closely packed
Together with
The rest – like the
Close segments of
A somewhat angular
Orange) shifts a
Little

Its position – feet and
Fold of wing – till
The returning
Sleepwalkers, settling back,
Hung up and
Folded, form
Part again
Of the still

Mass: of that
Dark, rough, silent
Bundle's skin.

*

At dusk
When the traffic again
Hurries out of town
And the light is
Changing – in the half hour
Between broad
Daylight and
The dark – I

Sat one evening
On a colleague's
Balcony, three storeys
Up, on the
Plateau: looking down

Into the exposed
Interiors of new flats
Opposite, open to
The air – and along the

Street a little
To where a
Flamboyant, long brown pods
Hanging, was
Alive

With birds. I counted

A dozen different species of a
Dozen colours (bright
Orange yellow,
Yellowish brown upon
The wing and back;
Black head with a white
Flash, the body
Ginger; gentle
Grey, smudged above
More darkly; fire
Red) – all sizes
From a thrush's

To that of
A canary – singing as

Variously and as bright as their
Own colours: hurrying
Off down the

Street about
Some business or other (soon
To skim
Back) in a small
Self important
Gang; and sewing up

Nests – these
The yellow
Weaver birds – with
Green pieces of
Grass string, disputing
Their possession, and
Abruptly vanishing
Inside them.

Beyond the trees and buildings
One could see an

Idyllic
Distance: soft receding
Horizon lines of trees – between
Which must
Lie concealed long
Stretches of
Lagoon water . . .

Above,
An immense sky
Was turning dusky
Blue, tinged with
Altering reflections
Of pink and orange
From the west; then

Becoming slowly,
Imperceptibly, lilac,
Lavender, and the
Deep
Blue of

Solid darkness, in which
All forms
Were silhouettes – while
The stars and

Moon,
Down low upon
One side of the
Aerial
Arena, showed
Silver.

From the town's
Centre behind me
To my left – moving toward
The unseen

String of irregular
Lagoons along the
Open Atlantic
Sea shore (folded
Down beneath those
Low lines
Of the horizon) ahead
And to my right –
Came

Flying (large

As rooks and more numerous
Than any multitudinous
Migration of starlings) – slowly,

Almost with a lazy
Tiredness, as though they

Had a long way to
Go, like

Flakes of
Leisurely, steadily floating
Ash, all in
The same deliberate
Direction, in

Ones and
Diffuse
Companies, spread
Over the vastness
Of the high
Skyscape (one flew

So low
You could see the
Exact shape
And the scale
Of it) –

Bats.

The bundles, like
Seed-pods releasing
Their myriad
Floating seed
Parachutes, were
Undoing
For the night.

At any time, over the
Whole area of
The sky, there must have been
At least a
Thousand; and they came
On steadily, quite silent,

From before I stepped
Out onto the balcony till
After I had left: three-quarters
Of an hour
At least. How many

Ten thousands is
That?

As the traffic
Scatters homeward, they –
Like flakes of
Accumulating
Darkness released by
The break up of the
Light – empty

From the town: flying
Where? For what? For
Fruit? For night

Insects somewhere
On the smooth
Lagoon surface – which reflects
And holds, gleaming,
All the slight
Light of the
Night sky?

Ignorant, I know
Nothing: only
What I see. The place
Presents, without
Comment, without explanation –
Quite matter of fact –
Mysteries such
As this
To me. The bats

Appear
There in the air
Before me
And have no
Explanation, no known
Meaning. But

In them
The meaning concealed
Within things
Is; you can
Open the door of
Meaning itself with
This new
Key: unarguably
Actual, authoritative,
Unfamiliar.

Light
Changes. And the
Bats migrate.

*

One evening on my
Way home, just
Before the bridge, I saw
Another thing less
Explicable even than
That general
Migration. There is

A monument
At the bridge end,
Tall as a
Factory chimney – one narrowing
Stone column, irregularly
Snapped off at
Its tip. And into that
Summit
Of the column
A single
Bat – wheeling
Purposelessly wide
Out above
It – suddenly

Vertically

Dropped. Then
Another. Then another:
Become present
All at once from
Nowhere
In the white
Twilight sky. And as
I passed on,
Another: several more. None

Came out. It was as though
Smoke, reversed,
Were entering the
Chimney.
Bat after bat

Circled near, flicked
Its wing
And was gone.

3

I rise too
Late to see
The bat migration
Fly back
In the morning, returning

To the town's
Centre – as I do to
My office
There. When

I'm about
It is established
Day already . . .

Having crossed
The bridge – on my
Route to
Work each
Morning – I pick

My way
Across the municipal
Bus park, among people
Standing about
Beside the great
Bus shapes, with their
Bundles; and stride,
Getting quickly
Hotter, up the

Hill,
Along the road
A little, and then
Diagonally across the
Open market.

Village maidens – from eight
Years old to ten or
Twelve – accost me at
The entrance, with

Bowls of little
Limes and of
Large loose-skinned
Mandarins, half green; and

Bunches of
Bright parsley
Like a posy.

Quickly when they
See you coming, if you've
Bought from them
Before, they run
For their small heap of
Produce where they've
Left it on the
Pavement (while
They chat
Together) and,
Rushing back, hold
It up – their faces turned
Up – toward
You: excited, amused,
Eager, sure of their
Reception, as though you
Were their
Papa. Appealing,
Provocative: difficult to

Resist, these
Daughters, these children
You can treat as
Children yet who are
Very much
Small women; slim as
Minnows, hardly
As high as
My elbow. It is
Like being in

A girls' school. 'You
Bought limes
Yesterday from

Her – why won't you
Buy my
Parsley?' But I can't
Use parsley! Then they

See someone else – a shopping
European's car slides
Up – and all are

Gone
In a moment.

So I get through
To the market
Square: where their
Mothers are, and the

Serious selling.

Heaps, feet high, of
Greenish
Oranges. And grapefruit, pink
Within, hard, with
A clinging rind, full of dry
Pith and enough
Pips to
Plant an orchard. In this
Damp heat these
Mediterranean fruits don't
Prosper. But there are

Mounds
Of formal
Pineapple – green
Again, and hard – yet all
Sweetness, freshness, all juice
Within as the knife
Cuts, rending,
Through the strands
Of the tender
Flesh's firm
Resistance; egg plant; passion
Fruit; guavas.

And avocados! I never knew
That these dark green
And purple narrow
Pear-shapes grew so
Big; or that, inside,
Their flesh could be
So deep for
The spoon's
Digging; or that to

Eat them ripe
You must, as with a
Pear, pick
The moment
Precisely: there is
In this heat a
Margin of
A few
Hours. They must
Be just
Not soft to
Pressure of the fingers.
Harder, they are
Like wood, soap;
Softer – no longer a
Firm or
Almost liquescent
Custard, but already
Rotting. And

Bananas! Heaped up
High as
A haystack, like the
Rays of an arrested
Sun: all sizes,
And a dozen
Flavours – the best, and
Most expensive, being those
Hardly as long as
Your little
Finger, like a
Small boy's

Penis (with a thin
Skin – and yellowish
Within, instead
Of the usual, faintly pink,
Cream white).

Many of these
Variously coloured
Contrasting shapes of
Fruit, bought on
My quick passage
Through the morning
Market – and carried
In my bag of
Etceteras and papers, slung
From my shoulder – I
Keep in
A basket on

My desk (the bananas
Piled up
Upon the spheres of
Citrus fruits – with a
Pineapple perhaps, to
Take home, standing
Sentinel, elegantly
Geometrical beside
Them), for anyone

To stay his
Hunger on; and to
Sustain
Me, independently
Provisioned in
My citadel
At midday, when everyone
Disappears to his
Hotel, or home.

Picking an avocado
For my lunch
Today, I make off – its
Grenade in one
Hand, satisfactorily

Heavy, filling up the
Palm – across
The remainder of the
Market square's
Wide

Space: heaped
With the bright and
Heavy brilliance
Of the moist earth's
Fruit – which women
Proffer me, as
If these shapes
Were what
Women ever have to
Offer us:
Themselves; as though I
Were being

Importuned
On all sides in some
Pressing insistent
Paradise of houris.

Here are cut
Flowers, frighteningly
Large, half as
Tall as I am: one
Tulip-shape and pink, filled
With fleshy pallid
Petals; another, a brown-
And yellow-spotted
Arum lily, bent
Back upon
Itself, resembling an
Open immense
Vulva, as large
As a handbag; and, more

Discreet, small bunches
Of yellowish white or orange
Stained, thick petal'd
Naked flowers of

Scented
Frangipani: all

Glorious in their
Exaggeration, their excess
Of form, size, colour –
Like the loose
Splendour of
The cloths the people
Selling them are
Wrapped in. I dare

Not stop to
Look at them or I'd be
Mobbed – with demands
To buy I
Have no time, or
Energy, to wrestle
With today.

Yams, the shape
Of some dumb
Burrow in the ground;
Coarse pots; and the

Woven exact abstract
Geometry of split
Cane, raffia and
Twig baskets – as pleasing
As if some intricate
Ancestral spider's web
Of thought had
Been fixed
In the air: precisely
Put on paper.

Women on
The ground (less prosperous
These, and older, than those
Confident off-hand
Princesses behind
Their great fruit
Mounds, heaped up

High on
Trestles) sit

Before their little
Piles of
Produce – wet brilliant
Lettuces, bunches
Of radishes arranged to
Look like roses, odd
Looking green
Tomatoes, roast groundnuts, and
Various pounded up
Cooked
Mashes – among

Puddles, flies
And the mounting
Market refuse. Small change

Is brought out,
Laboriously, from a
Knotted handkerchief
Somewhere in the dress, or borrowed
From a neighbour. If you want
Change for more than
The smallest
Size of note
You must ask the

Men at their neat
Barrow-stalls selling
Cigarettes: they, evidently,
Are richer. To get

By, I have to
Plant my feet
Carefully between
The piles and
Stride, almost, over the
Old ladies
Squatting (with their
Children, or
Grandchildren)

On a mat
Beside them.

The market is
Like an exhilarating
Swimming bath – which
I swim across
To work.

4

Then again
Cars . . . streets . . .

A building
Stands – square, concrete,
Tallish – in an
Expensive sea
Of calm. I run up
Its steps to the
Branching
Corridors and

My office: to see
What's wrong today.

My French colleagues
Intrigue. One of the
Englishmen
Is mad: an English
Failing. Fortunately, I
Like him. Personal
Defects, however small

Their seed, mushroom out
Immense, tropical, in
This soil of
African confusion.

The African
Permanent
Secretariat of this entirely
African international
Institution are professional
Men, inadequately trained, without
Trained subordinates
Beneath them (which means,
Briefly, that nothing
You or I would take for
Granted
Works), divided by

Every barrier one
Can think of – French
Speakers, English speakers; Mohammedans,
Christians, pagans; whitish skinned
From North Africa, and brown
And black, including

Ethiopians (from that
Mountainous antique
Christian fastness,
Altered little since
Our own early
Middle ages, which unlike
All Africa
Else was never
Colonized
At all except, late,
For a few short
Italian years: aloof,
Rootedly
Traditional); and

Come from all
The individual new
Nations, to say
Nothing of the old
Indigenous empires
And unnumbered
Tribes
Of Africa.

Get
Down to work.

What is extraordinary
Is the amiability
Of everybody. That makes
Up for a
Lot – almost

For the dreamlike
Desperation that one feels

When everything, at
Every link, breaks
Down. To give

One instance, at
The very
Simplest level: the
Porter at the main
Door has been,
I find, on duty
Thirty-six hours; his
Night colleague did not
Relieve him
For some reason . . .

Since he may not
Quit his post, I
Feed him. At any
Rate it's nice to
Make a friend. (However

He asked me
Later, as
A friend, to bring him
Back from England a
Diabolical damned
Transistor.)

Twenty times
A day, say to
Yourself: 'Patience,
Patience. And compassion.'

IV

OUT TO ADJAMÉ

1

Enough of the week's
Work: of those

Office rooms
With their
Air conditioning machines
That make it hard to
Hear what's
Said and

Insulate us from the
Environment we're
In – from the very
Air, humid and warm –
Behind sealed
Cool

Glass: like a vision
Of another
World, of some
Far distant hardly
Actual thing.

Enough of that work
Which I, a reasonably
Good I hope
Clerk
Charlady, or
Mercenary scribe, must do
Because I need to
Earn and am
Paid for
Doing it (and paid

I may say
Handsomely, in the
Short periods I
Gratefully
If grudgingly
Set aside
For it – though

Why should I earn
Immensely more than most
Other people in the world?),

Whereas no one
Will pay me
Anything at all for
This: writing
Verse.

Enough of that difficult
And in
Its way
Satisfying work, which
Takes me out
Into the world (and
Out to
Africa) and gives
Me beside my
Sustenance a certain
Position in
Society – so that
I can, not only

Hold my
Family up, young and old, as
A middle aged man, the
Man in the middle,
Must, but
Also
Say: 'This is what I
Am – an international
Civil servant
Scribe.' Though that

Of course is less
Than half
The truth. What

I am, the core
Within, is this
Man
Writing this . . . or

Escaping – it
Is Saturday
And now
Lunch time – from the
Entanglement, the confusions and
Frustrations, the tightening
Web, of the week's
Work. Exhilaration! To

Get
Out (while one
Has energy
Left still to
Enjoy it, to like
Existence
At all): to get out

And away! Far
Enough away
For the whole
Accumulation to
Slide off, leaving

One clean, innocent,
New (like that
New nut
Dropped from high up
On a tree
Overhead, which
Rolls along the
Pavement at my feet), naked,

Undefended
Before the open
World. So today

Let's get out
To Adjamé; leave
The week's work
And see what's

Over the edge.

2

It's hot. The
Sun stands

Still, in
A whitish
Unclothed sky, immediately
Above us – bearing with
Its full weight
Down – in the

Quiet of
The Saturday siesta.

Beyond the gardens
Of the square (where tall
Trees drop
Negligently, onto
The pavement at my
Feet, their
Unnamed enigmatic
Nuts, smooth, the size
Of a small
Walnut, slightly oval, and
Streaked – dark brown upon
Pale brown – with the
Moist
Markings of a serpent: dumb,
Shut, potential)

Quiet roads
Decline
Toward a cliff,
A one-track
Railway (down along the
Cliff base) and

The port. There
Large ships
Lie, in the lagoon.
And logs (as long
As the longest
Lorries I have ever

Seen, made expressly to
Haul them
From the bush, and thick
Through as
Antiquity) float

Awash – to stop them
Splitting when the
Dry season
Comes – making a wide
Floor out from
One stretch of
The shore.

*

Abidjan is the
Largest port of all
Once French
West Africa: shipping out
Timber, coffee, cocoa, fruit –
And bringing in to
This country and
To the ex-French
Territories inland those
Industrial goods which are
Their dream
Of affluence: a cruel
Dream, by which we
Hold them. Whence

The city's
Wealth. A wealth
Still French. For all the
Businesses of
Much account remain
In the one-time
Colonial masters'
Hands; so that
'Ex-French' is
More a courteous than
An exact
Description of this
New country – and the rest.

'Whose town
Is this?', an
Ivory Coast colleague
Asks me at
The airport, looking round
At the crowded lounge
Where everyone is
White – except for a
Few, like himself:
Who do not
Look at ease.

While an Ethiopian
Colleague tells me
That in the single
Sophisticated cinema of
The town his,
When he goes
There, is the only
Black face
Present: he might
Be in
Europe. And

If he wants a
Haircut, he
Has either to
Take the risk of
Getting lice, he says, in
One of those African
Side-street street-side
Barber's
Shacks, where people
Meet to

Talk and
Put in time (advertised
Outside by a

Board showing in
Profile, painted
By an amateur

Engaging hand, various
African styles of
Haircut – 'The Cock', 'Ghana-style',
'Tahiti' – all sculptured in
Solid hair,
Topiary-fashion), or –

As he does
In fact – go to a
European
Barber: unused
To cutting, and disgustedly
Unwilling to
Cut, this
Negro hair. Sophisticated

Barbers, like
Expensive cinemas,
Are for
Europeans. It gives

Him some
Malicious pleasure
To make the displeased
Frenchman learn his
Place and cut – this
Time at
Least – negro
Dense crisp
Wool. The pleasure

Even makes
The price
Worth paying. (If a
European has
A hand in the
Transaction you must
Multiply the price of
Anything by
Between three
And ten.)

Whose town
Is this? The French

Have command of
Everything – ships, shops, factories,
Plantations. Who
Can, exactly,
Blame them? And who

Change
The situation? However,
You can't expect the
Africans to
Like it. They
Don't. Though

They do like
Getting rich – helped by
These same Frenchmen. Who get
Thereby still
Richer.

*

The quiet side roads
Decline to
The lagoon, between

Gardens full of
High trees, heat, and tall
Shrubs and creeping plants in
Flower (that creeper

Whose light
Purple-blue and white
Flower bell is
Flattened at the front
Into the surly broad
Face of a toad, like a
Snapdragon – and

Allemanda, its
Butter smooth great
Flowers, on the bush, of
A bright pure

Yellow, opened back
Without seam from a
Wide shallow
Trumpet, appearing to be
Blank, without sound, without
Sex, at
The centre): gardens

In the still
Silence
Of midday, threaded through
By small neat
Birds, brilliant
Coloured, which make
Their small
Sung comment.

One tree has
Shed its leaves; and large
As a half
Sheet of
Newspaper these
Rustle on the
Ground, in
The imperceptible
Stirring of the air, louder
Than paper, as loud (so
Dry they have
Curled up) as
Sheets of foil: disturbingly
Metallic. Another,

So dark
Green as to be
Almost black, has leaves
As hard flesh'd and
Thick through
As a rubber
Plant's growing
Indoors at home, but
Closer set and
Larger: regularly
Placed like those of
A deliberate, mathematical

Verbena. This
Swarms like a

Vigorous
Sculptured nest of rejoicing
Feathered serpents – boa
Constrictor size – over
An area of garden: obliterating

It with its unfolding
Of immense leaved
Exultant
Darkness. While palms

Stand, clear
And high.

Across these gardens'
Space – softened by
Occasional shrubs and
Pillows of
Creeper and bamboo – tall
Trees raise
Thinner foliage, high,
Stranded in the air. And

In an underwater
Coolness of
Dark shade
An African family
May be seen – servants
Perhaps – half sleeping,
Stretched out on their
Mats, or squatting
Side by side upon
A bench, or stools, in the
Full stunned
Silence
Of midday.

A young woman, seeing
Me, wraps a
Cloth, seemly, across
Her bare

Cool breasts, as one would
Draw the curtain of
The family living
Room against the
Glance, from a public
Street, of some
Chance stranger: shutting me

Out from her warm
Home world, in which
One goes bare
Breasted, undefended, without
Formal disguise.

So too we
Europeans shut
Her out – from that
Glass and concrete
White man's world of
Power and money in
Which we
Are at home.

*

From the side roads
With their gardens
And view
Across the blue width
Of the lagoon, I

Stroll out
Onto the main
Road – now beginning to
Wake up for the
Afternoon – and
Stride off

Toward
Adjamé: waiting for
One of those
Free-enterprise small
Buses – or

A municipal
Big one (which
Stops only at the
Indicated
Stops – and is more
Crowded, and
Less frequent) – to

Overtake me.

It will be good
In the bus's
Shade to
Put the weight
Of the day's heat
Down. It is as
Though my

Hat
Were holding the whole
Weight of the assaulting
Silent
Sun up – as I

Walk on
The sandy ground
In the still heat
Of the air.

3

A great pallisade
Of bamboo
Leans out, above bare
Sidewalk earth and
Solid shade, half way
Across the
Roadway. Here
A municipal long
Low bus –
'Adjamé'
On the front – is

Approaching as
I approach the
Stop: stuffed
With people. Fed
In, I see,
From the back . . .

They include
Now
Myself, just.
Standing I cannot
See out of
The window, except
Downward
At the roadway, and might

Be in a tunnel – as
(All windows open) the shaded
Air, cool
Like a flowing
Stream of water, is
Forced briskly
Past us by the
Blessèd motion.

The smell
Of negroes: so much
Pleasanter, so much less

Rank, than
Ours. Here
At the back (I can get

No further, and pass my
Fare – long armed – over
Heads to the
Conductor), most of
Us are

Women: who hold themselves as
Well as they can
Upright as the bus
Jolts, baby
Heavy on their
Back: small,
Slim, with
Thin-boned, fine
Forearm and fingers.

(Seats go
To the strong: right
From the beginning
Of the run – when first the
Waiting, vigorous
Impatient men
Swarm in.)

A bright cloth is
Wound, loosely,
About each
Woman's head: so that they
Are like heads of
Flowering clover
Among the stiff erect male
Grass. While down
Somewhere at their
Feet there is a

Bundle,
Basin or a coloured
Plastic basket – pushed, for
Safety, up against
The bus side. Their

Babies do not seem the
Worse for
Being roughly
Brushed past, as
People at
The stops, pushing,
Struggle out. Limply at

Home wherever
Flesh is, they are borne
Up upon the
Sea of it (even that

Exposed head – above the yielding
Body, which is like
A pudding in a cloth)
Comfortable, companionable: safe

Somehow as
An internal organ
Protected still
Within.

This
Should do. The
Compact mass, reluctant,
Lets me
Go – together with
Several women, their babies and
Baskets – and
I am shelled

Out, like a
Seed on
The new earth,
On the sidewalk: more
Or less where
I want to
Be – near the

Middle of Adjamé.

*

That – across
The wide
Roadway, peppered with
Crossing people, through
Whom ploughs
Determined
Intermittent traffic –
Will be the
Beginning

Of the market: or
System of markets,
Rather, I
Should say.

Stalls at the
Kerb edge, selling
Clothes, shoes, watches,
Haberdashery, are being
Uncovered by
Their owners
And flowering into
Life again, after
The siesta; while other
Vendors squat
Upon the ground, their
Wares spread out
Round them.

I let myself
Stray loose, through the
Hours of
The afternoon: as a seed's

Roots – all bright
Sensation in that
Dark adventurous
Nourishment – branch through the
Intimate minute

Living structure
Of the soil.

Behind the street stalls
Are the acres
Of the open-sided
Concrete, covered
Market; and beyond
That again

A wilderness of streets
Lined with one room
Sewing shops
And houses: in the
Thick of which is
A further

Market yet, of
Rickety trestles and rough
Awnings, on the
Bare earth.

There – arranged, more
Or less, in their
Categories – is to
Be found almost
Every everyday
Object that a human
Being can
Use: from meat, fish,
Fruit, to cloth

And clothes – the clothes
Making
A hanging house in
Which, somewhere, the
Vendor is, concealed
Like a spider.

Beyond that
Yet again
The streets grow
Vaguer, the houses along
Them are like a

Broken-down dry
Stubble, and – withdrawing

Indoors only
In the heat, or rain,
Or late at night – life
Goes on, all of
It, out in
The open: publicly
In the streets
Of this
Unending

Village.

Eventually the dusty
Lanes lead
To a one-track
Railway – which people use,
On foot, as
Throughfare to
Get out of the
Maze: as in rough

Country
One follows
A stream bed.

*

A dusty, dense
Life, of people packed
Together, without apparent
Privacy, like a
Cake of dates – and
Confined
To the narrowest
Of horizons . . .

But how
Wide are
Your horizons? And what's
In them? What

Is the point
Of your life – of this
Life we all
Of us, here, are
Living: of
Any life? Have people
Found some glorious
Purpose to
Existence at

The Hôtel Ivoire – where
There is no
Dust, and one has
Peace, space: one's
Own large
Private room? Is
There a purpose
To be picked up
Somewhere on
The new clean
Carpet of the room I
Had there, stretched
From wall to wall?

There is one in
This
Dust. This is
Human: is substance,
Is the
Basis. While
That carpet

Is nothing – nowhere: up
(Half a dozen
Concrete empty
Storeys up)
In the air.

Here is dense close
Living: riches. Suffering
In plenty (but why

Not?) Suffering – and
Something. There

In that hotel, is no
Suffering of this
Sort, and people have
Got – God help
Them – what they are

Looking for: an empty
Bright clean
Box.

*

As children
Stand, now toward
Evening, in the lanes
And soap themselves
All over, carefully
Down the body – naked
And slim – standing
Before their
Half full
Buckets; and women, as

Dusk falls, bring out
Their small displays of
Fruit, and eggs, and bits
Of meat on skewers for
Grilling over embers, and squat
Down – chatting interestedly
Together – for the
Evening, side
By side (a cloud of
Children close
Around them, the small ones
Stepped over by
The careful
Passers by), and light those
Miniature storm
Lanterns that
Create a homely
Nursery world, half yellow

Light half shadow, far into
The night, tending
Their wares with that delicate,
Gentle, long, light
Gesture of the fingers; and men

Sit together in the
Narrow yards, or lie
On mats
Before their houses – silent
In the dark or
Quietly
Conversing – or range
About abroad
On their affairs: in

These packed-together
Streets where one
Has children,
Relations, neighbours, some
Sort of
Customary life, love
In its
Varieties, and

Work even if
One is lucky – who
Would say that

This, here
In Adjamé, is
A poor
Existence? There

Could be a
Better. But
Who has
Bettered it –
And by how much?

However narrow the
Horizon may be
That's seen from these
Side streets, humanity

Lies in
It. And for
What under wide heaven
Would one give
That away?

4

Out beyond
Adjamé the road extends
Through a broken

Countryside of
Bright green
Felled bush and patchy
Cultivation: where
Villagers thread their
Way down
Paths soon
Swallowed in the green – and

Pad along
The hard, red
Sun-baked earth of the
Road side.

Where the land
Folds down, and
The road dives
With it, suddenly a
Width of
Water, white and blue,
Appears; and

Between that
And the road lie
Washed clothes
Drying – a field of
Diverse bright
Rectangles – spread out
Upon the earth and grass.

Here, at a petrol
Filling station – where lorries,
With their unimaginably
Large loads of
Two or three
Gargantuan

Tree trunks,
Stand – a
Road strikes

Off upward
To the right
Into the wall of

Solid forest which has
Closed the view on
That side since
We left the streets,
Like the breakers
Of a besieging
Sea: between

Which and the sea
Itself the town of
Abidjan, with its
Spread out
Suburbs,
Floats.

The forest, rising
Up the slope, is
Like dense
Moss: solid
Underneath and displaying,
Above, varieties

Of greens, of leaf
Forms, branch forms
And of tall trees'
Tower heights, among

Which are the neat
Loose stars
Of palms.

This is what – all
Round, on the land
Side – the town has
Pushed away; and
What will roll

Back, springing up
Again where
This city stands
Today, once the
Human life, now vigorous,
Taut within
It, weakening
Grows slack: a green

Still
Sea – wave upon high
Wave of it
Out over
Horizon and horizon – breaking

Here in
The oceanic
Breakers of an
Abrupt
Forest edge.

*

As I walk
Into it, the green
Sea (its depth
The smooth tall
Tree trunks)
Close about
Me: and I

See, not
Now the lit
Leaf surface, but (all
At once) still,
Dimmed, the
Within
Of this forest
Water world – as if
I were now
Under water.

The bright patch
Of the point at
Which I entered
On the road – like a white
Water surface – pales

And, as the road
Curves, is
Extinguished.

I am in a
Tall tunnel,
Cathedral height: in
A solidity of forest
More dense
Than the human life
Of packed
Treichville or Adjamé. An

Even, stilled, cathedral
Underwater light. And
Silence. Not
An insect. Hardly the
Creak of a bird – up

High and away to
One side
At some distance. Only

Straight stems of
Great
Trees, which make
High islands
High up
In the upper air; stems

Slimmer, but as straight,
Whose leafage,
Lower down, cuts
Off one half of
The light; and,

Dense as fur, the
Stems of
Small scrub
Undergrowth, which one
Could – treading
The forest floor's
Leaf mould – scarcely
Push through.

It is as though I
Had scared the
Fish, the life,
Away. No animals: no
Animation. Myself and

Trees and trees: stems
And the underneath
Of leaves – seen mostly
Dark against
The diffused light
Filtering through
From the heights

High up above
Us like
Clouds, billowing
Up toward the concealed
Sun.

The yellowish green
Gashed leaves of
Monstera deliciosa, the
Size of half
A newspaper swarm, from
Unseen beginnings, forty
Fifty feet up
The tree
Trunks, upon a
Serpent stem
That roots
Into the bark. More modest

Philodendron, mounting,
Throws out
A smaller, darker
Shield-shape
Of leaf; and drops down

Into open
Areas
Of air, suspended,
Thin threads which
Feel for a
Fresh point of
Purchase (budding
At the tip) to swarm
Up from
With a new
Spring of life.

No other colour
Than these
Greens: no
Flowers at all.

Stems around me; leaves
Above, and lower
Down wherever
They can
Catch the light; with

Creeper threads (and
Threads of tree
Roots growing from
Trees' branches – exploring,
Slack like an untied
Rope) hanging
Down.

I have no
Language, no vocabulary,
To describe this
Solid, varied,

Road-pierced world
Around me: so
Shall be

About it, as
It itself
Is, dumb.

Eventually I
Swim
Back, out,
Up to the
Surface once

More of
The forest edge.

*

Before I turn to
Do so, after various
Twistings of the
Smooth unaltering
Uncommunicative
Road (an African

Or two walk
Past me – one well
Dressed, with his
Girl – and an occasional
Old car
Passes, dark faces inside
It, as startlingly

Noisy
As if it were
A speed boat: jolting
Me back all at
Once into a
Trivial, safe, familiar
Life – the depths' silence
Effaced
For the moment by that
Disturbance of the surface)
At one point

The vegetation
Thins, air lightens, a fresher
Green appears, the bare
Road branches and down the
Right hand
Fork a neat

Village is
Seen, its huts
Militarily clean.

A party of
Quiet women, and
Children trim for the
Weekend, are
Encamped at
The edge of it. The

Children, led by
One or two small
Girls, come out
At once, with smiles, to
Beg

Money from me. This tract
Of virgin forest is
Protected – and these
Will be the secure
Forest workers'
Families: who
Should know better
Than to prey, as though they
Were in want, on
Visitors. I am

Disproportionately
Annoyed – taken by
Surprise, emerging from
That silence – and give the
Girls my by now
Well worn
Paternal, affectionately testy

Lecture: which, though their
Mothers, Frenchless, would
Not (sitting a little
Way off, entirely
Unconcerned), some
Of them should
Understand. One girl,

Plumpish, wearing a
Clean pink
Satin dress
And small silver
Earrings, her hair in
Careful spikes, as
I pass back
Along the road
Again out of sheer

Impudence returns to
The attack ('Monsieur! Tu
Me donnes un
Cadeau?'), from a safe
Distance, simply to
Annoy me and put my
Lecture in its place. Liking

Children, I
Doubly
Dislike, as with this
Girl, being made
Not to; and that

Insultingly insinuating
Spoilt voice – she wins! –
Stings.

*

Beside the village, between
Long walls of green, a shallow
Light green pool
Stretches away, dimly, shadowed,
Out of sight – its perfectly
Smooth surface full

Of the forest's
Dark reflections (the air
Above it soft
As though it
Were misty) – calm and
Still: entirely
At peace.

On its far, reedless
Shore a woman, up
To her ankles in its
Coolness – and
Wound about by
The brightness
Of her cloth – stoops

To fill her
Round pot
With water.

INTERLUDE

AMIN ABDULLAH

A mile say
From the centre of
Adjaméd
Is a suburb

Of new flats: very
Spacious and set out
Among gardens, for
Africans of the
Professional
Middle class – less

Spacious of course and
Less expensive than those
Of my European
Colleagues, further out
Still, up on
The hill
At Cocody beyond the
Hôtel Ivoire: which
Have lifts, and
Seem set
In the free
Sky itself, away

From everything except
Ease, peace, luxury – on
An affluent abstract
Cloud, with a
Grand view
Of the distance.

In these new
African flats
Live some of
Our African
Officials: whom I get
Gradually to
Know. A process

Which takes
Time. For, since

They come from
A continent of peoples
Quite different from
One another – as well
As being different, all
Of them, from
Me – each has to
Be given my
Whole self, my entire
Attention. No easy

Thing on
Either side given
The pressure of our work.

However, one evening, only
One hour
Late, Amin Abdullah
And I (he seems,
As the few effective
Africans do, to work
Twelve
Hours a day) escape
From the office into

The street and a
Taxi. To these African

Flats, as to
The European, there is no
Public
Transport – the idea being
That, once you've got a
Flat, you've joined
The extra-terrestrial world
And have, like wings, to take
You to those
Clouds in heaven, a
Car, of your own,
Too. He has

None. Yet. So
We take a taxi.

I had asked him to
Have a drink
With me: having liked, as
I worked with him – for
A month or
More – the patient
Amiability, the quiet
And sweetness, and efficiency,
Of that young man
Of thirty,
Six and a half
Feet tall: his face
Courteous, up there
In the air
Above me – round
And smooth – on a body

Slimmer perhaps even
Than his impersonal, official
Discreet suit (African officials
Are required to
Wear suits,
And ties) suggested
That it
Must be. And he

At once cried
Out that he had
Been upon the
Point – now work
Had a little
Lightened – of
Asking me to
Dinner in his
Flat: would I
Come
This Thursday? His

Was the larger, if
The later,
Invitation; and he spoke
With a warmth

Which consumed him so
Wholly – burned up the
Air between us
With such
Hospitable joy, in
Anticipation of the evening – that
I could not cut
The occasion down
To a mere
Drink, on my
Ground: so I
Gave in, and

Went. Knowing
Nothing about him
At that time, not even
Whether he were married.

*

Out
We drive. And
Dismount: in
Darkness. Up

Flights and flights
Of steps – new, wooden,
Half open to
The air – long leggèd
Both: and stop
At the top.

He likes these
Flats, he says, although
Africans are
Noisy and, since you
Have to let air
In, you cannot keep the
Noise out. He has

Been here
Now (extravagant
At last) two
Months.

A small, pleasant
Room or two, with a
Great view
Of darkness, deepend
By distant
Town lights. New

Furniture, which
He has bought, quite
Tasteless: a black
Ebony head, pseudo-African,
Of the kind that's
Made for tourists, stands
On a special bracket
High up on
One wall. The
Artificial leather
Of the chairs is
A shrill
Displeasing green. Taste

Does not translate
Into a new
Culture. No doubt he
Would furnish
Differently, in his own
Way, at home.

He sits me
Down, with a
Beer – he, though he's
A Muslim, has one
Too – and we
Talk: for about

Three hours.

Upon which, when
I say I
Should be
Going, he protests
That I must eat the
Dinner that is ready

In the kitchen (I had
Thought the bits we
Had been nibbling from
A plate beside us
Were the
Dinner – though
I'd seen a table
Laid for two
Behind an alcove
Curtain); I
Cannot leave him
Without

Eating! So we
Eat, I
With knife and fork
(I cannot, though
I ought to be
Able to by
Now, eat
Stew
With my fingers), and
Talk, and I

Stay till
Midnight –

Murdering my next
Day's work (thin
Sleep I'll have, and
Little). But it's
Worth it; and even
If it were
Not, for me, I'd
Stay up all

Night to prevent
His feeling slighted.

He opens.
So do I. This, this
Is living. Let life
Afterwards look after

Itself – I shall
Survive
Somehow. He could

Not know, and I
Hope now
Will not, that – nearly twice
His age – I have
The oddity of
Needing, badly, a
Great deal
Of sleep.

*

He is
Sudanese – and has
Worked here
Several years. I'd

Thought his English
Perfect, it sounded, what
I heard of it, so
Natural; but I discover
Now that the other's
Speech can, for each
Of us, be very
Difficult to follow. And

Struggling to give
Expression to the furthest
Thoughts he can half grasp
Down at the bottom
Of his mind in
Darkness, he entirely
Fails to find
Words, sentences – even
European
Concepts – to fit
Them. He

Returns to the
Same point (the same
Idea – what is

It?) again
And again: each time
From a different
Angle, to try to
Pin it down – to show
(After a new
Sweep out into
The air and
Swoop) just what
It is
He means. Or

Rather, just what the
Question is he's
Asking. For the whole
Evening consists – apart
From my asking
Him, and his
Telling me, much
About himself – of
His questions and my
Attempts to answer. He

Wants to know, now
That he has
A European – conversable,
Open, warm,
Affectionate – before
Him, who he can
Speak to (he says)
Like a father, what I
Think – about
This, that, another
Subject, yet another: and
Back now
To the first.

Can you see
Then, a little
More exactly, what the
Question is
I'm asking?

The conversation
Is not without its
Pitfalls. For example

When I said
That as a young man
I did not, for twenty
Years, when everyone
Else did,
Wear a tie, he
Understood
(How?) that
For twenty years I
Had not

Played the guitar: and
He brought his
Own guitar
Out, to give me the
Pleasure now of
Playing one.

I think that what
He wanted was to
Learn, from
A westerner – well educated
(Omniscient indeed, almost,
As he thought me), someone
Who had lived, and learned,
And thought, a man of
Wisdom as an
Elder should
Be – at once

What way
The world was
Going today, and what
Life
Itself meant: expressed in

Terms that he could
Understand, brought up

At the other end
Of the earth
Almost from
Myself, in a mud
House – hut –
In the Sudan.

I held
The keys: to knowledge
And to the
Possibility of
Discourse. I had wide

Experience – so it
Seemed to
Him – and in that
Inaccessible, never
To be approached
West (which he
Part censured and part
Desired possession
Of with a
Lust of
The understanding), and
Thirty years of
Life's
Learning on my side lay
Between us. I was

The source: to
Which he lifted
Up, respectfully,
His appreciative
Pitcher.

I have not often
Felt – though touched,
And pleased – so
Small. There he

Sat (he had
Changed when
We came in) in a white
Long robe, like
A nightshirt, whose loose

Sleeves he
Could hitch up to the
Shoulder, waving his

Arms – of an impossibly
Long, elegant, black
Thinness – saying: 'I am
So happy, so
Happy. I
Am so
Happy.' And asking yet

More questions.

Early on I had for
Instance referred to
Contraception – I often
Do in
These countries – and
The plain arithmetic
Of the increase in
Our human
Population (a thing to
Terrify anybody
Who can multiply a
Figure, for every
Twenty-five years, by
Two); and what I

Said he
Took in – a solid
Block of
Fact – digested, and
Advanced from later to
Ask (filling in some
Gap in the great
Loosely woven
Fabric hanging in
The background of his mind,
Invisible to me) another
Question.

But exactly what
His questions

Were, as the evening
Went on – and whether or not
I told him
Much to the point
In the form he
Wanted – even
Now I do
Not know.

However, something
Or other, both ways,
Communicated.

'I am so
Happy; so happy.'

               *

Amin's parents
Keep a minute
Shop – of the kind,
I imagine, that I
Shop at here – in Khartoum.

He left school
Early, because as
Eldest of the children
He felt (his father
However, he says, did
Not) that he must
Start earning
Quickly to
Help keep
The rest. Since then –

Often doing
Two jobs at the
Same time, and studying
At night – he has
Kept going his
Father's shop, and supported
Two brothers and three
Sisters: paying for
The sisters' wedding

Parties (of three
Hundred people
Each) and for the
Brothers' education.

A few months back
He began to
Spend a little on
Himself: changing
His single
Rough room for
This flat. And this

Summer, when he goes
Home on leave – for a
Month – he hopes
To meet some girl
Who suits
The family (as she
Must), get to
Know her (unusual
This) and
Marry. All
In a month.

Having already
Bought his
Family a
Bigger house, he is now
Saving up for
One for himself, near
To them. His

Mature life
Can begin.

He has, I remark (so
A westerner must
See it), borne
With admirable
Cheerfulnes a very
Heavy burden. He
Does not see it
Like that: it was
Simply (this said

With no emotion
Whatsoever, merely
As a fact) his
Duty.

So – as I, close
Questioned, impart
What wisdom I
Can find for him
In me and in the
West – he describes
For me his

Family (the whole ramifying
Network of it, living
Close together) and
Life in

His city: where all
Immediate neighbours are the
Family too, and walk in
To one's small house
At any time, and
Eat what the household
Has, or
Nothing if
There is nothing. To

A wedding
All the neighbourhood
Comes; and the most
Remote branches
Of the family, from days'
Journey
Away. These
Live in the house and in
Tents put up
Outside it, for three
Days, until the
Feast is over.

This, all this,
I say, we
Have not: have

No longer. And, with
Pride, he allows
That that's
A pity.

Each, from his own
Side of the world, attempts
To show what he
Knows is
Precious in it
And the other
May admire – even
Desire

To possess
Himself,
In his own country. If that
Were possible: for
The virtues of the
One side may
Exclude those
Of the other. The nearest

One can come
Perhaps to
A wedding of
Two worlds is an
Affection such as
This is: this
Exchange between
Us, this kind of
Half comprehended
Conversation.

As between man and
Woman, between our
Poles of
Culture, and of age,
Life
Leaps: taut, complex,
Bright, burning up
The night as we
Strike deeper, further out,

Dark into the
Dark – until

We tire.
Midnight. Despite
The food, and beer,
I sweat
With fatigue.

*

Conversations
Somewhat similar I had
With a colleague
Amin's age, but
Very different, in
This same
Block of flats: an

Ethiopian I have mentioned
Earlier, much
Better educated, and speaking
An English like my own.

You would have thought that
He and I could have got
Closer to each
Other than we
Managed, in the
Event, to. He has
A dry
Mind, with a pleasant
Edge to it. But Ethiopia

Is more remote by far
Than its neighbour the
Sudan. Or perhaps
It is that
Amin and I are an
Unusually
Neat fit.

We were talking,
The Ethiopian and I, for

Example about
Sex. 'I do not

'Understand', he says, 'all
This that I read
In the papers about the
West's "sex
Problem". "Sex" is
What happens
Between a man
And woman: how
Can there be
A problem?' Things

Do, for
Him, seem
Ethiopianly simple.

'When my father' (a
Small landowner)
'Leaves home on
A journey of
Some weeks, my mother
Picks him a
Maidservant
From our house: to
Go with him, look
After him, cook and
Keep him
Warm at night.' 'What

'If the woman
Conceives and
Has a child?' 'Then
My father – he is
A good
Man – may
Adopt it
As his own. We have

'You see
No
"Sex problem".'

'And the woman?' I ask, 'can
She then, later,
Marry?' 'Female

'Family servants, in a
Household of our sort, do
Not marry.'

I see.

What sexual and family
Life, and life at
All, is like
Among the poorer
People in
His country he,
Like any other affluent
African – or well
Off westerner – has
No idea at all. He
Has no
Interest in
The subject – and,
Looking across the table
In a stunned way as
I speak, can hardly see
That there is anything
To see in the
Direction I
Am pointing. 'And

'What happens to those
Servant women's
Corresponding
Men? What do they
Do for
A woman?' As I with
Amin, he cannot
See what the
Question is
I'm asking. So, soon, I

Leave the subject.

Perhaps what makes
Conversation easy
Between the Ethiopian
And myself is
What, at the same
Time, keeps us
Most apart: his
Gentility – which gave him
A conversable, sophisticated
Western education. To be of
His class in
Ethiopia is to belong

To the feudal
Hierarchy of an
Antique era
My imagination scarcely can
Conceive of, and my
Sympathy won't
Stretch to. He sees

Things simply – within a
Framework which is,
Inhumanly, anything
But simple: in
A cast iron
Cage, the more

Disconcerting, in its
Rigidity and limitation, for
His command of English.

Amin, coming from a
More ordinary class
Of people – though one
Extraordinarily different from
Anything I
Know – has ground in
Common with me
Since closer to

The earth all
Share: however hard
Our words – and
Worlds – may be
For the other to
Understand.

Perhaps too
What draws me more
To Amin is
That he is more
Modest: aware,
Like a wise
Man, of the immensity
Of what he
Does not
Know. Simple
Himself, he knows
Nevertheless that
Things are
Not simple. While above

All, what he
Offers is no
Iron
Mediaeval cage, but
Something yet
More ancient: humanity, the
Heart itself.

*

Contrast that
Ethiopian
Attitude to sex with
This account that
Amin gave me of
His initiation.

In his middle
Teens, egged on by
Friends, he visited a
Prostitute – in her
Hut at the town's
Edge. As,

Screwing up
His resolution, he
Raised his crook'd
Finger to knock upon
Her door, she
Opened it and,
Forefinger
Crook'd through
His, gently
Drew him in – taking
Charge then of
Him (and on
Visits later, till she
Judged it
Time to stop) like
A mother: winning the
Boy's
Affectionate respect.

*

He stands
There now
Out on the roadway, while
We wait for
My taxi (still at this
Time of night they coast
Outside the town), a white

Pillar in
His shift – which is
Looped up (baring
The black
Arms) onto the
Shoulders – like
A tall woman (I can
Hardly
See him) in a
Ball dress
And a stole
After an evening's party.

A new moon is
High up among the
Few stars of
The sky, lying on
Her back – the thin
Points
Upward, like a balanced
Cup, full of the
Pleasures of the evening – in
Equatorial
Abandon. Good

Night! When
I am back, next year, in
Abidjan – and you
Perhaps are
Married – we
Shall meet, and

Talk again.

PART TWO

I

HÔTEL HADDAD

1

Stretching an arm
Out from this high
Window you could

Almost pick the
Mangoes (ripening,
A blush of orange
On them already) as they
Hang down
On their long
Strings – the size
Of a flattened oval
Cricket ball – among the
Thick

Foliage, matted
With what I take to
Be the old
Cocoons of
Caterpillars, and looks
Like dusty cobweb

*

After some time, as
Abidjan and I became
At ease with
One another
And I dug in
Deeper, I changed

My hotel: to
One in the
Centre – in
The thickest
Of the solid
Mass – of
Treichville, on l'Avenue de la
Reine Pokou: the Hôtel

Haddad. And that (three
Storeys high, it stands
Out with a few
Other buildings
Above this
Single-storey thoroughfare's
Roof level) is where

I am
Now: three storeys
Up in the rough
Concrete building, at the
Back.

Building blocks are
Piled up on
The landing by my
Door, beneath a
Ladder leading
To a flat part
Of the roof, which –

Open to the close
And changing sky
(Washing laid out on
It above the town
To dry) – has been
Left in part
Incomplete. They must

Have lain there (beside
A dead tap)
Years: the hotel
Letting these rooms

Meanwhile as usual
To its
African
Clientèle. And charging a
Stiff enough price
It seemed to me. But it
Is the cheapest

Hotel in Treichville
At which you can
Have that
To me
Paradisal

Luxury, a room
To yourself
Alone: a personal, private,
Privileged, unfair
Empire – precious as one's
Own separate
Body, as the free

Silence
Of one's soul.

*

The place is staffed
By various African
Young men – boys
Some of them. Dressed like
Everybody else, they might be
Anyone whatever
Dropped in from the
Street, for all you
At first can
Tell; and spend
Much of their time
Out on

The pavement, with
Guests from the hotel
And passers by
(Indistinguishable
From the rest – till
Gradually their
Faces grow, as they
Recur,
Familiar), blocking
Up the open
Entrance doorway: from
Which a slot, narrow

High and bare, like a
Coffin, or the opening to
A tomb, leads straight
From the street pavement to
The back of the building and the

Mysterious stairs.

It is owned by
Syrians – who have a shop
In front, and a couple of
Living rooms
Behind. One overhears

Their family
Conversations as they
Dine, in a room one
Half of which is
The bottom of the
Stairwell.

In the evening
Behind the counter of
The shop two
Middle aged Syrian men
Play, absorbed, some
Game on a
Chessboard. A young
Syrian woman, and her
Small children,
Serve. You hear

Her voice, raised, in
The morning, as she
Directs the
Hotel
Servants: who are also
Her own
House servants. I doubt
However if she
Herself
Ever enters
The hotel's

Rooms (she had a
Very vague idea
Of what, by way of
Furniture, there was – since
A few years back – in
Mine).

           *

A unique thing
About this
Room at the
Haddad is that
It has two
Windows. Facing east

And north, these
Look down over
Three-fifths
Of Treichville – and even
Out, away, over there
On the horizon
To my old
Antagonist
The Hôtel Ivoire: a

Hundred yard high
Matchbox
Stood on end . . .

On the lawn before
The Ivoire, seen
Even from here, a
Tree
Stands: immense, though
(Measured on the ruler
Of the building's
Storeys) little more
Than half the hotel's
Height. Its trunk,

Down at the base, forms
Buttresses, radiating out
(An elephant-skin
Grey) like the folds
Of a gathered
Curtain – as I

Remember from
My first night in
Abidjan when, fresh
Arrived and perforce
Lodged there, I wandered
In that hotel's dark
Garden, among its various
Equatorial superb vegetable
Excesses, on grass
Which was
Secretly
Sparkling with glowworms.

(The buttresses start
From two or
Three times my
Height, and gradually
Splay out
As they near the
Ground, making
A star-shape – pyramidal in
Profile – propping the
Tree
Up: each space

Between them being wide
Enough for another
Tree to
Grow in – here
One did – or for

The hotel gardeners
To use as a
Tool shed.)

All the Haddad's other
Rooms are
Windowless: with
Instead of windows
High holes
In the wall out
To the outer
Air – which,
Though they conserve
Coolness, prisonlike
Shut out the world; but
Not, naturally, its
Intrusive noises.

In this room I
Have both private
Peace, and (filling
The open windows, spread
Around and
Intimately
Below me) the
World. So –

Magical impossibility
Which we all
Aim at –
I have it
Both ways.

*

Outside, as I
Say, are
Mangoes – here in
The middle
Of the town. And

To a small tree
Growing up in a
Foot-wide space
Between the blind
Backs of two

Buildings, come
Doves, grey brown, almost
Pinkish (finer,
Much, than
Our pigeons), also

Smaller birds – some
Of which make their
Quiet
Comments heard
Above the sound of
Traffic from
The other side of the house
(Here that is
Muted, like an agreeable
Distant sea). While

In the great framed
Area of sky,
Miniature
Swallows, very sharp, wheel
Close – printed
Black
Against the light – in a
Flock, and quickly
Whisk away.

Below is
A low roof of
Asbestos, piled
With a bleached
Decade's
Rubbish: onto
Which mangoes
Drop, neglected, and a

Vine
Climbs, from
A courtyard hardly
Room-size in which another
Syrian family, from the
Shanty-like
Shop next door, spend
Most of their
Waking life: sit about,

Eat, wash, and pass as
In a sitting room
The evening. This family

Apart, the entire
View, as far
As the Hôtel
Ivoire, is entirely
African: Africa.

I might
Be up on a
Tree branch
In the forest.

*

The room's
Inhabited by, beside
Myself, an agreeable
Plump faced
Lizard, about four
Inches long; a black
Furry-legged
Spider, roughly
The same size; and
Ants so
Microscopic you can
Hardly see they
Are ants (cockroaches –
Very large – live only
In the shower). There are,

As I had
Heard, here in the
Thick of the town
No
Mosquitos. Though something

Or other bites
Me, every day, on
Some new selected
Area of
My body. Not

Bed bugs: the bites
Are not that
Blotched shape.
I never do

Discover what
The creature is, or
Where I
Collect it: perhaps
Walking over grass, or
Sand, in the
Evenings? Huge
Bites they are, left
By that
Invisibility: and lasting. And
They itch.

2

The other side
Of my room's thin
Door is the
Wide landing – upon
Which you find

Africans
Sleeping if you
Stir out
In the night or
Early in
The morning: stretched
Upon the tiles, each on his
Mat, a sheet
Over the whole of
Him, head to foot.
Quiet, secret. You can't
Tell who

They are: odd people
From outside
Perhaps, or some of
Our house boys.

From the landing
A passage leads, past other
Room doors, toward a
Balcony
Along the lively
Street front.
Through this passage

Air
Always blows, cooling
The house within. And

On it, toward
The balcony, on the cool
Floor sit
Usually hotel
Guests: a small

Party say of young
Women, come out
From the darkness
Of their rooms, half
Dressed – as people
Below sit out in
Their courtyards – some

Wearing that high
Headcloth which sets off
So well, beneath, the
Smooth clear
Features of the face; others
Abruptly

Bareheaded, unrecognisable
If you first
Met them
Turbaned (as though
They had been half
Beheaded, suddenly all

Face, all large
Loose features, beneath
The low
Small skull
Of closely
Growing hair teased
Out in spikes). This lack
Of a headdress

Makes the face appear
So near
You – above the
Slow-moving lazy
Body, in loose clothes
Which just
Manage to lap
Round it – that you
Almost

Back away.

*

My first evening, as I was
Settling in, a light
Knock came
At my door. Come
In! I unlock the

Door (one has
To lock it, or it
Won't stay
Shut) and there
Outside is

One of those young ladies: most
Personable – her headdress
Just up to my
Shoulder, and the loose
Freedom of a world of
Welcoming young
Rounded flesh
Below. We exchange
Names, pass
The time of day – and she
Strolls about my

Room, like a
Strange cat making
Itself at home: looks
Out at the view
Outside the window.

'Is there anything that
I can do
For you, this
Evening?' 'Well, I've

'Got, as a matter
Of fact, everything
I can
Think of that I
Need

Already. It's very
Nice of
You though. And
Very nice to
Have met you,
Madamoiselle.' We

Shake hands
At the door, and she
Is gone – all friendly
Amused smiles and
Darkness – out into the
Shadows of the landing.

What would
You
Make of that?

*

A few evenings later
I had given up waiting
In the passage
For the shower (it's always

Occupied by guests – or, often,
House boys – doing their
Washing up, or washing, in the
Wash basin,
Which takes minutes
To fill, or down squatting
On the shower's
Tiled floor: one tries
The door again

And again, returning, aware
Of the other
People in the passage
And inside their half
Closed room
Doors, who may or
May not be
Waiting for it
Too), and I

Had gone back
Finally to my
Room
Defeated – when another

Light knock came and there
Stood the same
Young woman, this time
(I could just
Recognize her) without her
Headdress. 'Come on, it's
Your turn – quick:
Va te laver!'
And thanking her – surprised,
In haste – warmly, I
Found the shower door
At last
Open . . .

I rely upon that
Shower room not only
For washing off
The day's heat
In but – as the
Others do – for
Washing up, and washing
Clothes, and for my
Drinking water: eventually

You arrange your day
Around the times at
Which you find it's
Likely to be free . . .

So her first visit had
Been, perhaps, pure
Friendliness, neighbourliness,
Curiosity.
Nothing else. Though
After all there was
Another service
A young woman

Might offer one on
One's first
Night in a strange

Hotel. There stood
My bed, taking up
Nearly half the
Room's space: a large
Statement
On the empty
Silence of
Its page. And
Treichville is

Full of tarts (dressed
Beautifully, full
Of superbia and
Self assurance) wherever
Europeans
Are: the town's a
Port, flushed

Through with
Foreign sailors.

Never imagine you
Know what rules another
Person
Lives by. Observe
Your own, whatever
They are: then
At least there
Is some
Solid ground. For even

If bed had
Been her
Intention, as it may
Well have
Been, indeed was
Probaby (there are
Tarts enough, relaxedly
Amateur, and
Some professional, in this

Hotel), she fell in
Easily enough with what
Was, she found –
On putting a tentative
Toe out to
Test the ice –
Mine.

While supposing
Bed had been what she
Intended, how could
I have guessed
Exactly what was
For her the point of the
Encounter: how much
Friendliness would get into
That bed and how
Much desire for
How much
Money? One is

At sea – on the small
Raft
Of oneself.

*

Something similar had
Happened at my
Previous hotel.

One day, walking
The streets of Treichville,
I found a small
Bar, rough enough, that
I could (here
Such things are
Uncommon) sit
In. A

Coca Cola cost
Three times as much as
I should have
Expected. However,

I drew a stool up to
The open door, to look out
At the people passing
In the street, lit
My pipe and (with a
Sense of
The divine
Emptiness, of immensity,
Behind me) grew
Absent.,

After a while I
Became aware that the
Waitress – slight, young,
Very pretty – had sat down
A little way away and
Had started
Talking: it was, for

That bar, the idle
Time of day. I found it
Hard to understand

Her particular
Variety of French. But
Searching round for
Things to say I
Discovered she liked
Dancing – and had been
Indeed one of the
Six girls who had not
Long since toured
The West
With the 'Ivory
Coast State
Ballet'. (I had
Missed it
When it came
To London: the girls had
Danced bare
Breasted, naked to the
Waist; and
The reviewers had been – that
At least I

Did remember --
Charmed.) She told me

Much, of mild interest,
About dancing
In the Ivory Coast, the
Company, its collapse, and
Her life
Since. She had
A 'husband': who I
Supposed to be the
Owner

Of the bar – but
Learnt later was
In fact
A student. She knew no
Word in French for
Fiancé: husband
Perhaps-to-be.

When eventually I
Got up to go
She seemed
Disappointed. 'Where
Are you living . . . what room
Number? I know, I
Think, that
Room . . . I shall call
In on you
One evening.' I
Said I'd be

Delighted; my wife
Would be most interested to
Learn more, from me, about
The State
Ballet. She on
Her side added that
She'd just be
Dropping in for a
Few minutes – to say
Bon jour. We each,
It seemed, had made

Clear our
Intentions. But

Had we? Passing that
Same bar some days
Later, in
The evening, I found it
Shut – and beside it the
Entrance to one
Of Treichville's
Night clubs. The name
Of the club, 'L'Ambiance',
Was written up, above
The bar – I had not
Noticed it – right
Across the house front. Hum!

On the evening
That we had – before I
Left – appointed, she
Arrived at my
Hotel entrance in a
Taxi (her bar
Was just round
The corner) and I
Entertained her

On the balcony
With beer – apologising. It
Was all I had.

She sat – dusk
Quickly
Deepened – and our conversation
Went on decorously as it
Had before. I found she was
Working in that bar
While her fiancé – who, she
Insisted, next time she
Must bring to
Meet me – was
Being trained
To be a
Chef: after which

They, if they both still
Wished, would
Marry. And
She was there
In the daytime
Only: at six o'clock
The bar
Shut, she went, and the
Rest of the establishment
Opened
As a night club.

She was a gentle,
Sweet and slightly
Silly girl – such as
Might, from a good home,
Have gone to a
Dancing school
In England. She asked me

If my wife could get
For her, in England,
Something she had bought
In Paris (Paris!
London! Europe! the bright
West!) and could not
Find in
Abidjan. A certain
Brassière. The make? The size?
She fished under her

Black
Jersey – and brought out,
In a matter of factly
Modest way, one
Of black lace. Size
Eighty-two (eighty-two what?) Her
Breasts were
Not very large – so
Big – she said, with
A sketching gesture
And an African
Entire absence of
Embarrassment (and with some

Pride: here smallish
Breasts, unusual, are
Prized).

After a while – it
Was quite dark by
Then – she asked my
Leave to
Go. I sat, waiting
For her to rise. Then
Realized, when she
Asked again, that
I – as the
Host, or the man
Perhaps, or
Her elder – had to
Rise first and
Release her. I rose. She
Thanked me, shook hands,
Went; and
I found her
Another
Unnecessary taxi.

What she might have
Made of it
Had not all
Of me been
Given already
To my wife (whose bed
For me is
A lifelong
Commitment – and deeper
By twenty years of
Married riches
Than any other
Woman's could
Be, so that
In any case there is
No great
Likelihood of
Competition) I
Don't know. Each

Changes the
Other. So be

Yourself and do what
You want, yourself,
To. Don't
Speculate too much
About what's
Being offered to
You. You'll

Get it wrong. And everything
Then will
Be, and
Will go,
Wrong. As it was

Things were
Right, in
Their own way,
Between us.

*

Looking at the
Women walking in
The streets though, and
At these young women
I keep meeting
On the stairs, with
Their menfolk, and
Passing the time of
Day with in
The passage (where, half

Dressed in the heat,
Talking to her
Friends, one of them
At my approach will,
Out of politeness,
Cover her bare
Breasts: as pleasant
To my eye as

Are those
Mangoes), I cannot say

That, even if I had
No wife, no love at
Home, I should be
So desperately
In danger. For

However lovely the
Roundness of
A cheek, the liveliness
Of a full lipped
Face that
Flows over, up
Toward you, with
Dark
Light; however beautiful
These loosened
Breasts' ruined
Landscape, and strong the
Close suggestion
There below
Of the thighs'
Sea
In the heat: still, these

Women – with that
Gait, soft and loose, relaxed,
Languid as if they
Were walking
Through a heap of
Sand, aimless, undone,
Limp and slow (grateful though

Their quiet
Abundance – unrestrained and
Unreproving – would be
To the child
In one that one
Can just
Remember) – more

Remind me
Of desire
Than rouse it
In me. This dark

Flesh is
Too foreign: in
That darkness I
Do not know

Where I am.

3

Outside
One window
Is the neighbour

Syrians' yard (a
Kitten, which has
Clambered
Up the vine, lies
Asleep on
The low roof in a
Mango's
Shade) and other

Yards and roofs
Beyond: out
Far – toward
The unseen forest
To the north
Inland.

One neat yard
Has a small
Tree like a
Tiered umbrella
Framed in it, beneath which
A young negro woman
Sits sometimes doing
Her sewing: a simple
Picture, painted
By a child.

Beneath the
Other window is,
Again, the life

Of Treichville: side
Streets and yards (and doors
Open upon their
Dark
Interiors) becoming –

As the scene nears and
The eye, steepening its
Angle, penetrates
Between the low
One-storey
Roofs – increasingly
Exposed: intimate,
Enlarged.

Immediately below
Is a large
Yard in which

Crates of empty
Bottles are heaped up
Against one wall, and a dozen
Men or so
Sort rags,
Stack firewood, and iron
Clothes on one or
Two rough
Tables (next door
There is
A laundry): all

Orders – given by the
Head man, erect in his
Shift of
Palest lavender
Which falls down
To his feet – being
Shouted, even
If from just a
Foot
Away; also
Much of
The conversation.

Before I'm quite
Awake, late sometimes
Into the night, and at any
Time of day except
In the quiet
Siesta (when the men are

Sleeping in the shade
Upon the heaps of firewood), shouts

Mount up, excitedly, from
Several of them
Arguing – or is it just
Discussing? – all
At once and most
Articulately
Together (the sound
Rising steadily in
Volume
And in pitch, each cry
Clambering sharp
Above the last, dangerous
Sounding like a
Dog fight) about how

The work should be
Assigned, or done, I
Imagine; or the gambling
Game that they
Play at night.
They seem, most of them,

To live there: sheltering,
At the rare
Times when
Anyone needs
Shelter, in the big
Barnlike
Laundry alongside.

Next to that yard,
Below me, is
Another: bare, a few
Steps across, outside the
Back door of
A private house and
Extending round the
House side to
The street. There

Mothers move, bodice slipping
From the shoulder, about their
Household tasks – washing,
Cooking – or sit feeding
Babies at the
Mountains of their breast
(The small
Darkness of the baby
Obliterated by the
Weight of that
Night sky); and children

Naked, unbound from
The back, learn to make
Their initial
Unsure steps – on shaky
Diminutive plump
Legs beneath the great
Out-curve (arms out,
Up) of
Their belly.

In the evening
Men sit, too, on a
Bench at
The side of the
House, and exchange
Courtesies with people
Passing in the street
Behind. While

On the pavement of
That back street, backs
Against the wall, other women
Settle, on stools they
Have brought with them, selling
Fruit, and nuts, from
Trays on the ground
Before them – mild luxuries of
Evening – a group
Of four or five, comfortably
Together: each having her

Storm lantern that lights up
With its glow a
Cavern in
The night, of
Sociability, of neighbourly
Quiet pleasure, and
Ease – which also
Is commerce. They settle
Down together

Like girls sitting along
The wall in a
Dance hall: while – in that
Half dark
Back street – dark people
From this immediate
Neighbourhood (the hundred
Yards or so around) move
By.

*

Out beyond that,
Treichville
Extends, its
Rightangle streets
Packed with
The irregularities
Of life (whose intertwining
Obscures the
Streets' strict
Pattern): a maze

In which, walking to
Work, I get
Lost, led astray
Into new
Unknown worlds
Each day; and which

At night – here from
Above – is all

Points and
Planes of light, angles, shadows,
Revelations (its low down
Crowded privacies
Suggested by –
Everywhere repeated –
Lamps' and lanterns'
Lit up
Indistinct
Exposure), alive

Like a rock
Gleaming with bright
Mica.

*

Above – sheer
Up above my
Window, and out
As far as
Distance goes – is
The height
Of night: that black
Beyond us

Against which our
Lives (the little
That we
Apprehend of them) are
Lived, and into
Which goes

Each one
Of our loves – my brother
Last year, his son
This – and

In the space of
Eighty years every
Creature
Here now in
Treichville: even those
Who, like beans in the

Warm pod, are
Pressed still to
The close, obliterating,
Soft and heavy smooth
Pleasure of
Their mother's breast.

Where the lights
Prick, there below, lives
Enter: when the alert
Member, among dark hips'
Heaps of sand, leaps to
Light up the
Concealed
Cunt's storm
Lantern. They stop

A while here, in half
Seen, altering
Mysteries; and soon

Go. This is a
Railway station – a huge
Hall, all
Arrivals and departures: compounded
Of bright light, suggestions and
Pitch darkness. All alteration,
Change: today

A curtain lifting, and then
(What day?) for
You the great
Curtain

Coming down. All days
Then – and all this
Night too, now
Before us –
Out! Out. Out.

At any moment
You must leave.

That thought gives
Existence
Grandeur, its
True scale. Knowing that
You must go
At any moment, that any
Thing may
Go at
Any moment, gives each
Thing here

For you – and you
Yourself – the
Full huge
Scale
Of that: of that
Falling of the curtain.

You become, yourself,
Its size. It is
In you – who shall
Be (and are,
If truth be told, already
Now) in
It. So

The journey, the
Departure,
Is not all
That
Important. Only is

Vastness.

Live
That vastness
Here! See it
Outside the window – high
Above the lights and low
Roofs, above
The lives and packed
Domesticities and loves of
Treichville!

Since all this spread out
Below me, solid as the
Earth, beneath, itself
Is, may blow away
From me at
Any moment – a yet
Greater depth, annihilating
It, revealed – I settle down
Upon the scene lightly
Like a butterfly, looking
Round on all
Sides at the
Light, while holding

Yet
The darkness that
You are
In, my dead
Dear brother, in
Me: which shall

Be mine, be mine
Too to
Be in.

Dark or light, it
Hardly makes a difference.

Yet the absence that
Is now where
Once you
Were, stands always
Beside me: a huge
Space, nothing

About which
I understand.

*

Once, in the day time,
Outside one window the

Whole sky grew
Black, and without
Warning (I
Shut the window)

Fell. The rain
Sluiced down
From the sky, wetting
Anyone caught out
In the street, through, in
A few
Seconds. The mothers

Drew indoors, collecting
In no particular hurry
Cooking pots and
Children; and the streets
Emptied, except
Where people sheltered, in the
Freshened air,
Under trees and
Eaves. Slim

Children strolled
Naked; and in
The beer bottle and wood yard

Men, half stripped, washed
Themselves, busily, in the
Free showerbath
From heaven – which
Thus came to them
Without need for
A long journey with a
Bucket to the tap. One

Sat in a tub, and
Soaped himself
All over. Others brought
Out hand
Basins. And the whole
Yard, as the black
Sky fell, became a

Vigorous
Bathroom – which had

Been work place, restaurant,
Dormitory, debating
Hall and games yard.

The town was
Washed through
By the welcome
Wetness from the sky: a shower of
Life – of water's
White – in the
Obliterating form
Of flood, of darkness.

Fresh – it was
Soon finished. The last
Drops
Relented. And

Streets and yards – as
The precipitating tension
Eased, and the blackness
Drew back
Above the forest – filled
Up again with people: as
They had been before the
Heavy sky's

Invasion, before this calamitously
Life-renewing, thundrous, hissing, abrupt

Revolution: which left
For some hours after
In the heat a

City of muddied
Sand, and puddles.

*

Both windows open
My room seems

To contain – on
My return
At dusk – the whole high
Night air
Of the town: while

The town's life is
Spread out before
Me like a
Field of grass,
Full of intense insect
Complexities and privacies and
Flowers: which

I can survey from
Up here
Like a bird, or

Enter, an obscure
Rejoicing mouse – an enjoying
Creeping
Caterpillar – as

I choose.

II

STREETS

1

On my way out,
Leaving my room I
Pass on the
First floor
Landing a large

Kitchen table
In an alcove – on which
A young man, talking
To his friends (they have
Brought in a
Transistor),
May be ironing
Laundry – and

The hotel's shut
Office: through
Whose window
You can see the
Board of
Room keys. To get into

Your room when you
Return you have
To find
Someone (in

The passage, or among the
Knot of at first
Indistinguishable people – house boys,
Passers by of all kinds, hotel
Guests – silent or in
Desultory conversation
Passing the time upon
The pavement, blocking up the
Doorway) who

Can find
The head
House boy. He

Alone – in charge
Day and night, and
Flittering about like an
Amiable, quick, long
Leggèd lovely
Swallow – has the key
That unlocks
The office, with its
Imprisoned
Room keys.

He does most too
Of the hotel's
Work (including changing
My one
Sheet, and
Pillowslip: sometimes
Once in ten days, sometimes
Twice in
Two – and sometimes just
Taking one or the other
Of them
Away, leaving behind
Bare ticking).

I drop my
Room key in
At the open
Office window; move

Lightly (in light
Cotton clothes
And sandals – which
Interpose but a
Slight barrier between
The easy body
And the easy
Warmth of air) down the
Second
Concrete flight of stairs,

Along the slot
Of passage – high, naked and
Narrow like
A prison – and am

Out

In the street, opposite a
Cinema
And a small
Vacant plot, with
A public latrine
In it. At night
This is a
Market: dense
With people, in slow
Milling motion, and with
Darkness – relieved by
The firelight of braziers
And by rows of storm
Lanterns on
Trestles, behind which
Women sell

Fruit, roast meat, fish,
Eggs: every
Provision you
Might want
For the evening.

Everything – domestic life,
Trade, sociability,
Traffic – is going on in
The street at the same
Time; and most people
Seem to know many
Of the others
Well, as though
This were a

Village. A village
Of villages – but
With a metropolitan
Spaciousness, a zest

To it: an air of
Hope, change, freedom

Insecurity.

*

I am hailed
By one of
The group lolling in the
Doorway: an African
Fellow guest, who has been
Living here
Ten years – and sells
Antiques to
The antique dealers. Just back
From a few months

Inland, he has in
His room
Rough sacks and broken
Cardboard cartons
Full of masks, small carvings
And figures almost
Man height – broken, most
Of them, and eaten away at
Some time by
Termites: and

Broken more each
Time he dumps
Them out onto the
Floor to
Show me, or
A customer. Either
It has not occurred to him
That one can
Not break
Things; or he thinks
Brokenness a mark
Of authenticity: that it
Adds flavour – is a
Quality such things should
Have. Yet his

Objects are
Authentic: bought in
Those villages whose
Life once
Gave carving – gave
These carvings –
Meaning. Dying,

That life now
Releases
Them for our
Appreciation: whose culture,
Killing it, has
Killed with
It, at
The source, this
Sculpture which
We feel able
Safely to
Admire today . . .

Even I
Have, here,
Acquaintances! Another

Antique dealer,
From the Plateau,
Stops me in the
Middle of the street – where
The lively motor traffic
Stirs up the pudding of
Pedestrians. In the course of

Our formally polite
Conversation I learn
That true
Antiques may not
Be exhibited
Publicly
For sale. Fakes
Only. Authentic

Pieces one shuts up
At home, or keeps wrapped
Up in newspaper beneath
The trestles, to bring out
Covertly when a sale
Seems likely.

And again, later,
As I am sitting in a
European-style
African restaurant, an African
Colleague comes across to
Greet me: each of us

Relieved to
Meet the other without
His disguise.

*

No affluent African
Like that would
Be seen, I may say, in
The restaurant
That I usually
Eat at – across the
Road, beside
A photographer's shop

That's full, all evening,
Of an enormous
Sound of
Radio, bright light
And people: attracted
In like
Moths. There

At a row of tables
Down each concrete
Side wall of a
Small cell

Open to the street, you
Can eat – alongside

A grave
Labourer or two, a young
Dog in
Sunglasses
With a pipe, talking too loud,
And a boy
In a torn shirt
Come in from
Begging in the street – a

Bowl of
Red and
Interesting enough
Stew, just not too hotly
Spiced to eat, with a heaped up
Great plate of
White and
Cooling rice, 'riz soupe'
(It costs
A few pence), brought out
From the back. As you come

In, a large loose
Girl (she has no
French – I speak, she
Grins) lays before
You on the board a
Lilac coloured
Plastic mug of
Cooled water (from
The icebox – the only furniture
In the room beside these
Chairs and tables), over which
She lays then
Delicately, crossed, a
Knife and fork.
On the wall hangs
One

Photograph: of
The President, Houpouet-Boigny.

People stay just
Long enough
To eat. I sit, and
Smoke: society, abundant, ever

Altering, is – all
Of it – out there a
Yard off
In the street.

2

The wide pavement with
Its punctuating
Tree trunks (whose foliage,
Unobserved above,
Casts down
Daytime shade) – its

Iron drums
Of litter, bedsteads
For sale, loose refuse,
Puddles, and
Women and children
Camped before
Their wares – is

Crowded to the sociable
Point at which
It is just not
Necessary to push
Past the
Dark people
Close about you in the
Warm, partly illuminated
Darkness, to get
By.

A tall
Old man – his beard sprouting
Bright white
Against the darkness
Of his face – smiles, on
Receiving alms a
Little larger than is
Usual, as though some
Personal exchange, not just
That gift of
Money, had occurred
Between us. And a young

Man, noticing
The gift, and the
Response, stops,

Surprised, with a congratulatory
Exclamation
Of approval.

On the ground small
Children, up against
A house
Wall, lie
On a rush mat or a
Piece of cardboard, quietly
Sleeping – a few feet
From their mother, who
Sits out on
The pavement at the
Close
Of her day. The calm

Abandoned faces, trusting, lie
There, where you might
Put your foot . . .

In a side street, as I
Overtake a group
Of girls out
Strolling, one
Of them (without French – except
For the word
'Cadeau') falls into
Step beside me, takes
The bag that's
Hanging from my shoulder
And walks on
With me, carrying
On meanwhile a
One-sided incomprehensible
Mocking
Conversation. I cannot,

Without fuss, get
My bag
Back – so we march
Along, all of us
Together, in
A phalynx: till we come

To a crack between
Two houses, leading
To a private
Narrow yard. She,
Entering, makes to
Draw me in. 'No!',
Laughing. 'And
Now I
Want my bag.' Then
She will keep
That, at any
Rate, as
'Cadeau': bantering – almost
Serious. I
Have, amused, to pull
It firmly
From her. How will

Her neighbours,
Standing near in
Evening conversation, take
This? I am
As to the rules of
This sort
Of solicitation (evidently
Amateur) entirely
At sea.

Amused too – they
Laugh. And
We all shake hands.

Yet further
On, I am accosted
Rudely (it is
Not however
Meant so) by one
Of a dozen men
Sitting together, backs to
A blank
Factory wall. 'Excuse me,

Sir' (he walks out
Toward me), 'could you
Settle a point
For us? Seeing you
Passing here several
Times, on
Foot, we
Have been guessing
What you
Are. Are you a
Missionary? A philosopher?
A teacher?' Not
Any of those,
Quite: a
Writer. Satisfied,
He returns to his

Wall; and we all bid
One another, acquainted now,
Good night.

3

Sometimes, among these streets,
I hear the
Sound of music, drums
Amplified, and – in

A backwater where
Are no dangerous
Dark forms of
Cars, bumping, too fast,
Upon the pavementless
Uneven roadway – find a

Mass of people
Blocking up the fairway,
Sitting, standing: while
Children, like starlings, are
Perched on
Window ledges, all quiet
Attention, to get
A better view.

Beyond the dark
Mass of them
Is bright light
And a space
Cleared – in which are

People dancing: great
Women, in a brilliant
Cloud of cloth, moving like
Slow mountains
To the beat.

Once, it was
Men and women, all in
Voluminous
White, dancing, each alone,
Slowly, remote,
Oblivious – as if
In a trance: like ghosts,
Or angels; arms

Raised up a
Little, the eyes
Shut; slowly

Swaying, with the whole
Body, as though they
Were floating, as
The music welled up
Through them, floating
Them out
Into some
Inner bliss. Those

Were, I was told,
Christians. And that
Was all I learnt.

Again – at the street
Corner next to my
Hotel, one night,
Outside a
Single-storey house
Of two or
Three rooms
Perhaps, someone

Gave a party. There were about
Fifty women. Some
Sat on two rows of
Chairs facing
One another across
The narrow pavement, drinking
Soft drinks (the evening
Crowd in the street
Beside them was
Already dense). Between the

Rows, others were
Dancing, in a long
Line, with hardly
Space to move
A foot – shiggling, swaying,

Crying out,
Laughing – to the music
Of a radiogram
From somewhere: no doubt
In the house. The sound

Went on
For hours – all
Evening. It

Was like a
Street dance on
Victory Day
In England after the last
World war. But
Here neighbourliness
Does not
Need war to
Bring it out. The pleasure
Clearly

Was immense,
Gargantuan, for
Everyone. Perhaps, since
That house, or the one
Next door (judging by
The school girls one
Saw outside
Them in the
Daytime), was
A girls' school, it

Was an old
Girls' dance.

*

But best – one weekend –
Was a dance
Across the road
From the hotel: on a
Vacant plot
Near the night
Market.

Floodlights lit up
The area; and
Standing people (children
Threading among them, underneath
One's elbow) lined, a dozen
Deep, the surrounding

House walls
And the end of the arena
Where it joined the
Already jammed
Pavement of the street.
The lights, beneath

The black of night, were
Like a tent.

Four musicians, at
One end, squatted
On the floor. Two had,

Each, a
Xylophone, some
Five feet long, whose
Broad cross slats,
Of wood, up
To a foot in
Length, gave
Out, struck, each
Its own
Graduated note. While
Two had

Drums, large
As a tub, made from a great
Gourd: slapped
With the hand
Or fingers. From
Each drum's rim
There rose flat
Horns of
Leather – vibrating – whose

Edge was threaded
With small loops,
Like beads, of
Wire: which rattled,
Jangled, bell-like,
Accompanying the drumming,
Like the rim plates
Of a
Beaten tambourine.

The musicians went
On, on – playing
Over and over again, with
Just the slightest
Variation, the same
Phrase, long drawn
Out, complex: which got
Gradually into your
Blood, your bones, working
Up till
You felt

Exaltation – and an
Admiration for
The minute
Mathematics of the
Passage: which changed
Hardly at all, but

Changed; and
Changing yet
Again, and
Again,
Repeated, made
Its effect.

For some time
The area cleared
For the dance
Was bare.
At a table

Sat what could only
Be the

Master of ceremonies: in a complete
Cowboy kit, of black
And silver; with a silver braided
Cowboy black hat
On his head, sinister
Dark glasses, a short
High jacket, fringed
At the edge, holster,
Spurs, and
Trousers clinging to his
Narrow hips – hardly
Wider than his waist.

A youth, in
Black pointed shoes,
Smoking a cigarette, strolled
Into the empty
Space, and up negligently
Toward the
Musicians, as though
He had no
Business there at
All: feeling
The music flood into
Him, feeling
For the moment. Without

Warning – standing in
Front of the
Musicians, alone
In the bare
Arena, cigarette
Dangling, the complete
Indolent insolent
Figure of
Ill health – he

Exploded, like a firework, into
A foot
Dance: so fast and
Intricate, following
Each half beat
Of the music as it
Reached its

Height, that
You would have thought
It impossible for
Feet, supporting that
Limp loose body, to
Execute such
Fore and back steps,
Hardly to be
Followed by

The eye, the
Understanding. Abruptly,

Burnt out, he
Broke off. And
The music ceased.

When it
Began again, two
Lines of dancers formed, one
Of men, the other of
Young women, and advanced to
Meet each other, from
One side and
The other of the
Floor: slowly
Shuffling – dancing
Scarcely at all. Anyone,

It seemed, could
Join in: some
Learnt as they
Went on.

A boy of about
Four, wearing a
Dirty singlet like
A nightshirt – to
His knees – drifted about
Among them, learning the
Steps
Too. And, perfectly
Solemn – to the indulgent

Pleasure of the audience, who found
Him quite in place – he joined

In every dance that
Followed: imitating
In his vague
Stray-dog
Way, even
The master of ceremonies
Himself (who gave a

Pyrotechnic
Exhibition, very brief, like
A rocket, almost
Rivalling in
Virtuosity the
Youth with the cigarette); and

When the floor was
Empty did his
Own dance, immediately in
Front of the musicians – who
Played on.

I heard them playing,
After I
Went home, far
Into the night.

4

At dusk, amid the
Sound of music, heard
Here and there in
The approaching darkness
From where people,
Unseen unless you
Chance upon

Them, dance (now
At the
Weekend) in the
Maze of
Criss-cross streets – among

This maze of
Individual lives and
Families, of tribes
And neighbour groups and little
Shops, and
Workshops hardly
Larger than
The shops are and
Still open – I stand

At the edge of crowded
Treichville where a

White bridge – borne
Up on high
Concrete arches – launches
Out over the smooth
Lagoon. Fires

Are being lit
Beneath grids at
The street side – roasting rough
Lumps of meat and skewered
Brochettes, for the strolling
People who
Pass by all the

Warm
Evening long – and women

Settle down
With their bundles, piles of
Peeled white
Oranges and
Storm lanterns, as
Though they were
Invited to a party.

Heads down, haunches
High in the air, Muslims
Are at their evening
Prayers, wherever
They may be
At the moment: back
To the sunset, bowed
Head to
The east.

Beside the lagoon
(At first a sheet,
Rippling,
Of silver) women
And children, near the
Water's edge – just off
The main shore road
That slips beneath the
Motorway where
It becomes
A bridge – squat

Shitting, as the ancient
Custom is,
Contemplatively, before day
Closes: becoming
Almost, as they
Squat there,
Silhouettes.

And hunting
Bats, striking out
Into their night

Empire, and
Homing birds, relinquishing the
Day (which of
The two is
Which?), mingle –
High up or
Planing
Low – against the

Pink and orange and
Deep blue-silver of
The sunset: above the
Lavender, turning
Soon to lilac, of
The calm space (never quite
Extinguished) of the

Night lagoon.

III

LAGOON

1

If you have time
Enough, and energy,
At the weekend

You can get out
Also
East, the opposite
Way from
Adjamé – immediately
From Treichville along

The straight, branching and
Cross-linked lines
Of road that fly out
Toward other
African more trim
Well spaced-out
Suburbs, to the

Slum
Village of
Port Bouet, to Grand
Bassam – an older
Capital –
And eventually
Ghana. To

Lagoon, and
The sea. Water: space!

Peace.

Immensity
Returns, as you look out
At that nothingness
Of water which
Occupies
Half of the earth
Before you: making

One clear
Line (all else
Cut away) of half
Of the horizon.

Undoing all form –
Everything that's
Made – water
Wipes clean, and

Creates us. The
Week is
Blotted out. I am
Undone, emptied,

Restored, recreated.

2

The shadeless side
Of the
Straight road is
Hot, and virtually deserted
In the Saturday
Siesta, as I set

Out: turning
Round every
Hundred yards
Or so to see
If, in the stretch of road
Behind me, one of
The cars that are,
From time to time,
Imprinted on it
In the distance
Is a

Bus. A little
Lorry, that is: with
A canvas hood
Covering the rib
Cage, and a battered
Tailboard that's
Hauled up – and held
Shut – with a
Chain. It will be

Full, inside, in
The aerated shade, of
Dark
People (faces, bodies,
Baskets – a great spare
Wheel perhaps in the middle
Of the floor space,
With people's bundles
On it) sitting on

A wooden bench which
Runs along each

Side, and on another
At the end, back
To back with the front
Bench intended
For the driver (onto

Which, clambering over other
Passengers, people scramble
Too), the conductor

Perching where
He can: on the
Tailboard eventually
When the thing's packed
Full.

Some of these small
Buses have
A legend, an exclamation, a
Cry, written right
Across them: *Du
Courage, Dieu Seul, Prions Dieu,
Grâce à Dieu, Dieu Merci,
Dieu Ayez
Pitié de Moi.*

As gay
As fleas
One or two appear, tattered,
Rattling, in
The distances: the first
(It does not
Stop) evidently
Full; the next

About to strike
Off left, to a
Suburb, Markoré, I
Do not want to
Go to; then
At last
One – with
Room in it – going

Where I
Do. I wave

Each down: if
Not full

It swerves in to
The side of the road
Ahead of me and I
Half run – out of
Politeness, shoulder
Bag bumping on
My back – declare my
Destination and get

In, up the
Let down
Tailboard. Or,

If it is not
The right
One, let
That fish escape.

Inside, the heat is
Gone of my

Long walk in the
Bareness
Of midday, out past scattered
Factories, villas, institutes, set
Among gardens full of
Trees – which yet
Do not extend their
Needed
Shade (it falls
Vertical) to me on
The roadside – beneath a

Sky of
Greyish white, half
Worn through by
The brightening, heart-lifting

Dangers
Of the sun.

A roof's
Above us (dark all
Together in its
Shade); and through the
Sides air
Streams, fast as
The bus's speed – as
Cool and fresh
As one might imagine
Air to be
In the furthest blue
Cool reaches
Of the sky.
Coolness dries off

The wet
Skin, revives the
Flagging dusty
Spirits, fresh as
A new leaf – among a

Thicket of
Bodies sitting
Pressed
Up together. A young woman,

Voluminous and easy, sits
Solidly beside me
In her bright robe
And a high
Headdress (my arm
Behind her
Holding the side
Ribs of the lorry's
Cage) alongside
Men in a white
Shift or a
Tattered singlet – our feet
Filling up the entire
Small free
Floor space – while

The lorry rattles,
Bounces, swoops to a

Lurching stop, and puts
Off again
Gaily, another passenger
Loaded up behind (trying
To find a place to
Put his feet, and his
Hands, as he
Climbs
Forward), and the view

Streams past the open
Sides, quick as
The passing air that
Is forced
Through us, and
Fragmentory
As bunting.

So I
Rattle out to the
Horizon in
The freedom of the open
Afternoon, the open
Weekend – away
From the city, from land
Even (half of it
Cut away), from everything
Of the little
That, in this
Place, I
Know.

3

About
Here: that
Will do. I can

Just reach to
Tap the driver – and climb
Out, paying

The conductor
On the way (he has not yet
Clambered about among us
To collect his
Fares: which the women –
When asked
Eventually – will
Extract, slowly, from the
Corner of a handkerchief
Buried somewhere
In their clothes'
Concealment).

One side of
The land-surrounded
Road just now was
Taken down and –
Beyond young

Palms – cool
Lagoon water
Stretched. I shall

Walk back to
That – picking up,
From the huts which
Among renewed
Vegetation have closed
In again the
Road, a heavy

Bottle of beer, to
Restore
The sweat I've lost, and

A handful of bananas: provision
For the day. One further
Freedom!

Several huts have
Beer advertisements, by
Way of decoration; and one,
Beer. Inside,
This is like a
Comfortable ancient
Packing case, with a few
Shelves and
A wooden counter, worn
To a blackish
Grey – like the loose

Pitted sand
Outside – grown grey
From the years that have
Been lived out
On it by the
People of
This hut
Hamlet.

The bananas – displayed
Upon a tattered
Grass mat outside on the
Grey black
Sand, with a few
Groundnuts – are offered
By the woman squatting there
Before them at a price
So low

That the profits from her
Entire stock
Could hardly buy
Half of this
Reckless luxury, my
Beer. Camped there
For the day – her world of

Neighbours and family
Behind her – she yet seems
Content: as calm
As the lagoon; and sparkles
Like sunlight unfolding
On the water with the
Unlooked for

Pleasure of the sale.

A few yards of tended
Grass bank – upon
Which young
Low palms at
Intervals
Rustle together the
Stiffly pleated
Fingers of their leaves, stirred
By the air (not
A breeze
Exactly) breathing
Off the water – lead down

From the bareness
Of the roadside to
Bare
Water (how
Different a naked
Openness!) stretching in
Every direction, smooth, out
Almost to the
Horizon: not in
Two directions
Only – linear, dry,
Narrow –
Like the road.

Ripples
An inch high
Lap in
And cluck against the

Sod which
Is the shore; and
From that

Stretches this
Wide sweet
Calm of
The lagoon – to where,
Far out along the long
Horizon, a further
Lagoon shore is
Seen, annotated with
Palm jottings, and

Silver suddenly
Where are the
Cylinders of
An oil company's
Tanks: the shape of those

Gasholders which brooded,
Iron, blackish, in my
Childhood, outside each
English town.

*

I sit, my sandals
Nearly in
The water: look
Out – think
Of nothing. A leaf of a

Young palm tree
Clatters against me, like the light
Spokes of a fan.

Upon the water's surface
There is nothing whatsoever, not
A ripple
Even, to the far off

Green furred
Horizon (a new

World – high up, seen
From this
Level – on which
One might one
Day
Land), blue

Only, changing to
Grey silver
As the sky
Changes (imperceptibly
Greys over, then
Again
Clears), varied

Everywhere and ever
Altering, yet
Without form, without edge,
Without any indicable
Transition between one tone
And the next. This is a

Liquifaction – is
The essential tincture – of all
Things: a liquid
Distilled reduction of
Them, without loss.
And looking at

It, at this
Blue then
Greyish silver surface,
I am
Reduced: reduced to one
Drop, an essence,
In a
Vastness – in a blank

In which
My being is
Enlarged, replenished:
Healed.

I think of
Nothing; and from the depths

Within, unseen, that
Life larger than I
Am which might
But for this
Elude me
Stirs.

Look out
At the water: be blotted
Out – and
Healed!

*

Another palm leans
Out above the water; and
Down it

Rustles a lizard, male, a
Foot long – more
With the tail – steel
Blue, stained in
Patches disconcertingly
Rust red. It checks

Upside down – near
Where the trunk's base
Clings at an almost
Horizontal angle to
The cut off
Shore – and stays

Still as a nail that
Has been
Driven in, head
Up, stretching the
Dry throat's octogenarian
Skin folds, looking

At me. I
Look at it: presented,

Confidingly, as close
And clear as
A jewel on the
Palm of the hand. And

We stay so
For ten minutes; all

Afternoon it
Might have been – but I
Moved my leg: and
Like an image
On water, broken, he
Was gone.

Meanwhile small
Lizards, greyish
Green (almost, as live
Shrimps are,
Transparent), fine
As needles, came out,
Went back – behind
The trunk or
Off into the grass: stopping

Suddenly as though time
Had been
Chopped off: then
Breaking the trance as
Suddenly (as if someone

Had touched the
Water surface of
What one's
Looking at) and
Rippling off, as
Fast as fish.

That male lizard
Stilled time to a

Stop: and at
The focus
Of the lagoon's
Lense
For ten minutes
There was his
One

Gem studded, jewel sharp
Image. Looking, I
Slipped, from
Mine, into
His life.

The water is
Transparent at my
Toe, to a sand-earth
Bottom – sullied
By a few bits
Of human
Debris (a sunk
Plastic bag), but
No matter.

On the bottom, the
Bottom of my
Beer bottle
Cools. The beer,

Like the lagoon, wipes out
The week: cools,
Like the lagoon, the
Heat the sun
Half released piles up
Upon the land. And as

Several hours go
By, passed in
This forming
Bud of
Things, in water-scented
Peace, I sustain myself

On one
Supporting
Island then another of
Tropically ripe
Banana: taken
From my bag.

The lagoon's
Unimpeding surface, like a
Sail, gathers every
Air there is
In the still day, from
Here to
The horizon – and,

Out of that
Vast
Bowl, breathes it
Into the
Palm fronds
Beside me: which, lightly
Clattering, fan
The day's stillness –
Freshened – stiller
Still.

Wading, to his waist, a
Fisherman comes
Toward me – black, muscular,
Male, against
The water's surface of
Grey white – and

In a cloud
Throws out
His gathered
Net: like a lassoo, a settling
Balloon, a puff
Of steam. Allows it to
Subside, sink; pulls
It in. Strides on

Further (reading as
He may the surface
Of the water), casts
Again. Nothing
Caught yet – he

Is gone, out of sight
Beyond rocks which
Form a screening
Promontory. The lagoon
Is still,
Featureless again.

This is the growing
Point within the
Bud
Of things: whereon
No image
Is, yet in which

The whole plant's
Future's forming. In

This, this stillness, clarity,
My being
Is. And
From here

It is but a short
Way on –
In – to
Where one might

Slip out of life.

4

The afternoon, thus
Suspended, could be hung
Up: never
Taken down. Yet

Ends: the horizon
Colours – as the sky's
Tent's
Struck: slackens, starts to
Lean. And I

Walk back along the
Lagoon-side
Road: to where
A European restaurant
Lets me sit

At a café table in the open
Air, sipping the luxury
Of one more
Beer – this time
Brought me by a waiter.

Shrubs – scarlet
Bougainvillaea, plump
Butter-yellow
Allamanda – lose their colour
And become
Silhouettes, shadows – as
On the lagoon the
Violence of
Silent light
Increases. Flies

Try, irritatingly, to
Share my beer glass and
Have to be
Waved away.
Mosquitoes' stinging
Near-invisible needles
Thread the air. Before

Me, beyond the garden's
Undergrowth – which
Receives me
As kindly as
The familiarities of
Home – a bank
Of vegetation, topped
By tall
Palms, stands
Against the lagoon
And the sky's low
Intensifying light.

Edgeless, formless, imperceptibly
Altering like the
Water's surface, the sky
Changes. Explosions of

Whitish light
Upon blue-silver
Strike upward beyond
The bank of palms
Over the whole huge
Height of the sky; and,

Immediately behind
That piled up
Vegetation,
Molten white light
Burns – turning

It, drained, charred,
To a black
Silhouette. The earth's

Life's
Gone – out
Into the sky; whose light,
Reversed, is thrown
Upward, up
Over toward the
Back of things: not down.

As the intensity
Increases, gains colour – gold,
A little
Pink – the earth,
And the sky
With it,
Shrinks. Look round

You a
Moment: everything is
Narrowed; the position, the place
Of things is
Indistinct. And

When you look back
At the horizon, there are
No longer
Explosions of the day's
Immensity – is no
Longer that volcano,
Vastness, but a mere

Monument
To the day:
Small, in
The undone diffuse
Approach of darkness.

I must go
Home – while I
Still
Can see.

IV

THE SEA

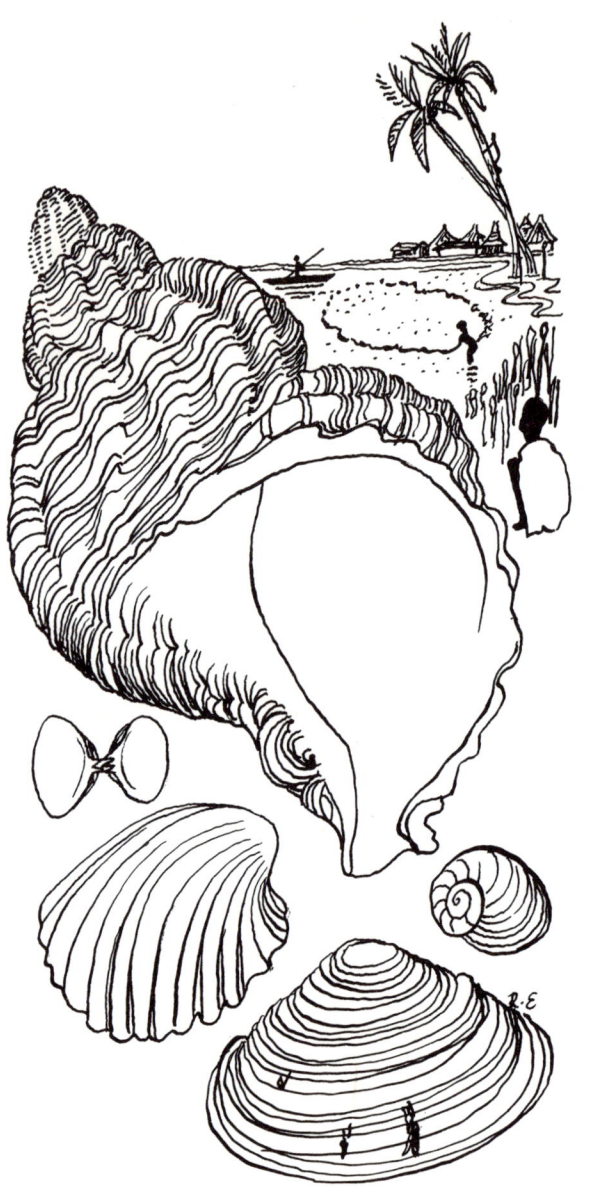

1

Another day – with the
Whole day, Sunday,
Before me – when the bus

I have waved down
Sways in to
A stop beside
Me on the
Straight stretch
Of sandy road – with its

Gardens, spilling their
Loose, abundant
Equatorial splendours (wide
Open hibiscus, and that
Creeper whose
Blue flower bell
Is flattened at the front
Like the flat
Mouth
Of a frog) – I ask:

'Port Bouet?' 'Port
Bouet!' I get
In. And

We rattle out
Further, along
The flatness: air streaming
Through like
Joy in the veins, a flag
Of holiday; tattered

Scraps of landscape,
Seen through the
Windows, and us
Passengers, all
Jolted up
Together.

The road becomes a
Low

Causeway, along
A neck of sand that
Cuts a lagoon
In two: smooth water
Blue at either side
Of it, tree-fringed
On each
Far shore. Next – where

Another road
Strikes across it, and
The traffic thickens –
It skirts a
Wide bare
Area of
Earth-soiled
Sand, littered with
A few dead
Tree stumps, and trampled

Over and
Trampled yet again by
Sheep, cattle, goats: which
Rest along the
Side of the road
In droves, their
Herdsmen
Beside them – among loosely
Scattered groups
And knots of other
Africans – or troop

Strung out
Emaciated along. People –

From prosperous merchants,
Mohammedan, grave, in
Their white long
Shift, to men
As tattered as
The bony herds
Are thin – are camped
Out in the open
For the day; while

Here and there rise
Temporary hamlets of
Torn sacking (without
Water, or sanitation
Other than the sand). Low

Buildings beneath
Green trees – a mile
Away across the desolate
Flatness, where vegetation
Again like
Life and hope
Begins – are the
Abattoirs.

The road
Thrusts
On – into the small
Shack town, the fishing
Village, of

Port Bouet. Behind those
Huts of thatch,
Old boards, mud and
Wattle on the
Right will
Be

The sea.

On the left, already,
Is a market. I'd
Best get
Off here – before the

Town, thinning,
Suddenly
Is gone.

*

Still now at midday
Along the roadside
Rough trestle
Stalls (and salesmen
Squatting on the ground,
On mats spread out
Upon the blackened
Sand) are selling
Cloth, shoes, new
Shirts, and worn
Clothes scrupulously
Patched. Behind them

The market
Is finished
For the day: stripped to
Its bare bones
Of rickety thin
Poles, haphazard platforms, high
Uprights for awnings – among
Piles of decaying
Fruit and
Vegetable rubbish which,
On the sullied
Sand, you have to
Pick your
Way past,
Among puddles: abandoned

To the inhuman
Vigour of the flies. These
Buzz, black, up in
All directions, swoop
Down, settle, and scribble
Their crooked
Flight lines over
Everything, blackening
Midday with
Unseemliness, decay,
Danger: as ubiquitous

As blowing soot, as
Dust, as the
Grittiness of sand.

A few women are
Finishing carrying
Their unsold
Wares away; and
Near the street-side
Stalls some
Clothes sellers
Sit yet,
Tented in their stock.

*

Trampled into the dusty sand
Of the roadside opposite
Are bits
Of fish, and extinct
Fish scales. There, and

In the vague lanes
Between the houses (which, at
Peace in this
Place, grow up
As a tree trunk
Grows, from the ground
To a dry
Foliage of
Palm thatch), the sand –

Yielding deep,
Disconcertingly, beneath
My feet – is
Grey black
From generations of
Human lives that have been
Lived out
On it: like the soft tilled
Black earth of an English
Cottage garden. And here

Is a dead
Rat: flattened
By car tyres to a
Piece of parchment – the first
Rat I've seen
Round Abidjan.

Elsewhere, what's
Flattened on the tarmac
Is large
Lizards, the size
Of rats – scavengers, plying
The same trade – caught
Out, for all their
Quickness, by the
Speed
Of cars; in their
Clicking movement,
Mechanical, checked
Now, timeless,
Once and for all.

Sometimes, they tell
Me, children
Are hit: as you'd
Expect, since this main
Motor road
Goes through the middle
Of the village – through
The middle, that is,
Of a communal
Nursery, sitting room and
Playground – and this

World of flesh and blood
And that dream world
Of engines, steel
And speed
Don't
Mix. If that

Happens, and you
Are driving – drive
On, they say,
As if the
Devil were behind. Stop,
To try to
Make amends (what
Amends?) and you
May be torn
To pieces by these
Quiet parents living in their
Huts upon the sand.

Then who'd
Be to blame? This

Village was
Here – people
Were here – before
The road and its cars
Came. Besides, these

Poor people
Do not, yet,
Play at
Cars – you'd not see
Them sitting,
Devoured, inside
One: become
Mechanized, a less
Than human
Sprite. It is not

Their game that
We are playing
As we plough
Through them.

Best not to
Mix those two
Antagonistic

Magics. So stay
Out.
Or on foot.

I walk
Through the village.

Outside, beyond a patch
Of sad newly
Planted coconuts
A lighthouse
Stands, out on the
Sea shore – among
Buildings which
Seem, dilapidated,
Now to

Be a school.

2

In a car (to
Break off here
A moment) you

Can – as I
Did once with a
European
Colleague – drive on
Beside the sea

Past many flat
Miles of
Regular coconut
Plantations, in strips
Along each side of
The road (a pillared wide
Cathedral world
Of exactly spaced out
Stars of
Palm fronds – tousled
Tufts, each
On its single
Evenly notched
Stem – at the centre
Of which swell, like
Pips in a fruit, the
Coconuts), in

An hour or so
Back
Decades to
Grand Bassam, a one-time
Capital – from earlier
Colonial days – now

Dead, allowed to die
All at once
With the rise
Of Abidjan.

Yellow ochre
Buildings, two storeys

High; pillared facades;
Space, a taste of
Strangeness – Spain,
Though Spain here
Never was. The buildings

Stand yet, for the
Most part: but their
Life is gone. All life

Is gone, except
That of
A village: quiet,
Arcadian, idyllic, among the
Cool Edwardian
Colonial architecture, the wide
Half empty spaces, palms.

Outside what was
A luxurious hotel,
Restaurant and night
Club by the
Beach, in a wide
Street between
Collapsing
Walls, a sedate game

Of football
Is in progress. (A very
Polite young man
Asks us
To move a few yards
Aside: we're on
The pitch.) The hotel's

Outbuildings have
Fallen in; the great
Room on the ground floor
Is open
To the world. You
Could if you liked
Rent the upper

Floor to
Live in – but

Be careful
Where you put your
Feet, and remember
That what was the
Lavatory at
The corridor end is
Space. Behind,

Filling up the end of
A cramped
Courtyard, by a stairway, an
Oceanic
Woman sits, calm as
The largeness
Of the sea, on a
Stone bench – half a dozen
Children round her
Like chickens
In the shelter of the
Fluffed out
Feathers of a hen. Not

Stirring, she motions – with
One immense
Soft arm, like a squat
Tree trunk – an older girl to
Fetch us
Chairs, from some
Room in
A ruin behind: we
Sit. And,

Civilities exchanged,
Enquire about the
Terms (my companion
Is a little
Interested) for taking over
Part of the
Upstairs
To live in. Wide

As the sea – she
Shines, black, with
Sweetness
And the heat.

The children, as we leave,
Make a
Polite farewell, each
Of them: wave; and
Return, small,
To the enormous
Comfort of the nest.

Back inland from
The sea, in the main
Streets, are
Half empty
Village shops; and village
People loiter, pass the
Time of day. Beyond

That again
The houses become
Farm houses: among
Trees, countryside. A

Gentler life has
Taken over, where
Once
Pride was . . .

The sadness
Of a death; dignity of
Great bones
Abandoned; and sweetness
Of the fresh new

Grass, low down,
That springs up
From the earth – out

Of each
Quiet crevice.

3

A little way past the
Lighthouse
At Port Bouet,
Needing a seat
And beer, I walk

Through the garden
Of a European
Restaurant, open
Welcomingly
Beside the road (it has
A swimming pool and
All the rest of it) and sit
Away from the company

Where a low wall
Drops down to the
Strand – and the sound

Of sea
Drowns all
Sound, all awareness
Of what
Is around me.

It is like
Sitting underneath
A waterfall, or
Entering the blank
Of meditation: which washes
One's past, all that has
Accumulated, all staleness, and the
World away.

A spray
Fills the air, salt,
In a faintly
Silver cloud, a mist
About me – flung

Up from the
Steeply shelving

Shore, where
The waves pound
In: making, it seems, the

Ground, our whole
Earth, tremble.

Twelve feet – fifteen
Feet, how
High? – without
Preliminary the rollers
Swell, round
In a full
Circle, like

A rising wheel, up –
Over, and

Down, pounding
In a froth
Of white
Foam on
The abrupt slope
Of the shore: sending a

Petal of
Flat hastening
Thin water, each time as
Confidently
Impetuous as the last, and
As ephemeral, up
The smoothed-out
Wet dark yellow
Steepness
Of the sand. Then they

Suck back,
Out – dragging coarse
Sand with them down the
Smoothed clear
Slope – and are replaced,

Even as the teeming
Rattle of their

Ruin
Returns, by
Overtaking

Others, which
Again
Round in
A pure
Arc: hollowed
Before the drop.

The blows are
As if of a
Felted
Hammer on
An anvil of
Hard sand – or,

In the distance, of
Cannon
Booming: unendingly
Repeated. One might

Be inside the
Earth's
Machinery: below deck,
Where the heart, the engine,
Pounds. Even

Some way off from
The shore, with each
Boom the earth
Shudders
Underneath one's soles.

Here an
Ocean
Ends – and one
Feels the leaning
Weight of it.

A log, from
Inland, cut for
Transport and escaped

Somehow from
Further along the coast,
Black wet, five foot
Thick and – it
Is short – say
Twenty long, is lifted

To the tidemark, almost
Holds there, and rolls
Back down
With the rushing
Backwash, further
Into the sea's
Ruin than it was
Before: wallows, on weaker

Rollers making
False essays, and then

Is lifted, end forward
Athwart the waves, high
Up onto the
Sand; holds there
For some waves
Further, till – washed
Half sideways to
The sea – it is
Sucked back
By its tail: returns.

How many years
Does this go
On?

Another great
Log, lifted by some
Quite exceptionally
High tide, lies
Beached, just touched
By the swirling
Skirts of water – sand
Around it, half heaped
Over and sucked away
To make a

Hollow at
One side.

The pounding, the
Repetition and dissolving
Obliteration of the water
(By which all is
Turned to
Smoothness, movement,
To a sliding
Remodelling of the sea's
Stuff and
The sand) dissolves

Thought, awareness, memory,
Within me: so that I
Become, within,
One
Vastness – one blank – one
Magnificence, the forms
Of which, changing in each
Particular, are not
Fixed, ever, for
A moment. I am

Loosened, loosed, relaxed
Entirely – by being
Made all
Movement. And washed

Fresh: wide
As the sea, great
With this
Unpetalling of the ocean
(Whose scent is
Salt, and whose
Bursting blossom the
White foam and
The booming) as

It occupies, muscular, in
Motion, the
Whole of me.

I seem, myself,
To have been
Washed up
By the sea. Vastened
To the size of
It, I leave
Myself here, and
Take

The ocean home.

*

Here three
Things are: calm
Of the smooth
Stretch of the
Horizon, which
Dissolves one half
Of the earth
Away, unbounded by
Any sight of
Vegetation or
Imaginable land; the pounding

Of this
Hammer of the sea,
Which reduces
Everything ultimately
To sand crystals between
It and the
Anvil of the shore; and

Coolness
Of spray – that moderates
The sun – and of this
Glass of beer, formally
Brought out for
Me: which, sipped,

Sinks like an hourglass.

4

At the other side of
A reed fence at
My side, are a
Few huts
Under occasional
Palm trees: outposts
Of the village.

I walk back
Toward home
Along the shore.

Firm land is
A high
Shelf, above the
Waves, composed

Of pitted
Soft sand – dry,
Full of shells
Deposited by the highest
Most mountainously
Tempestuous tides – and of

Peaty
Earth: into which
Is trampled rubbish and
Refuse from the village,
At this its back
Door
Onto the sea.

There are coils and
Broken stumps of
Human excrement: exaggerated
Bold statements of
Inhuman size. Even

Below on the wet
Roof-steep
Slope – kept smooth

By the repeated
Irregular washing of
The up-reaching
Sea – the same
Coils appear: swirled round
By the sifting, settling
Wet sand.

Here and there
A man
Squats. Or a
Woman or two
Stroll out
From the palm-thatch huts
And crouch down
Too, looking easily
Out to
The horizon. One has

To walk
Past them: neither
Noticing nor
Not, as though one were
As accustomed to the
Sight as
They are. This

Is their
Shore.
And the sea

Is the nearest thing
To a sewer
That the village
Has. (These people

Don't dig
Cess pits, in which
One's excrement is
Devoured
Instantaneously almost
By the grateful
Land: any more than
Our own villagers
Usually now

Do, who – like
The people here –
Flush in
Their case their sewage
Into the nearest
Limpidity of
Pure water, salt or
Fresh no matter, they
Can find.)

Walking therefore,
Even on the wet
Sand, you have
To keep
Looking all the
Time, to
Avoid the turds, forward
Down onto
The ground: away

From the constantly
Repeated altering violent
Ruin of the sea's
Wall
At your side; from the

Half of the world that's
Cleared, cool
Smooth and blue, beyond it
Right out to
The horizon; and from,

Before you, the long
Strip (topped by
Coconut trees and
Huts) of the
Sloping
Yellow shore.

*

The slope's so
Steep that, at the
Base of it, waves

Pile up upon
Waves' shoulders. They
Loom, swell, take

Individual shape, break
And, broken,

Sweep up the slope – to fall
Back at
Once, ruined, beneath
The towering
Swelling of the next. Nothing

On such a slope
Can hold
More than a brief
Moment: all slides
Back, like rain from a
Steep roof – back
Into the ruin of this

Two thousand mile wide
Ocean's termination, broken off
Here house-high
Beside me.

Upon the yielding
Steepness of the slope
My feet
Slip, sink
In – and I take off my
Sandals to get
A better grip
Upon the coarse, silted
Together wet
Particles of sand.
Coolness

To the feet! Which a
Wave, reaching out
Suddenly from
Ambush in
The others, wets
With the thin swirl

Of its skirt sent
Spinning and ruffling
Up the slope. Another,

Entirely unexpected, chases
Me up near the
Top of the slope and
Wets me to
The knees. As the cotton

Trouser dries, a white
Fresh tide line
Is left on
It. Salt.

*

Although the shore's
Too steep for
Swimming, boys
And young men – stripped, black –
Run down the slope,
In, and
Jump up and down

Shouting: exposed
By the water almost
To the feet, then
Overwhelmed, buried
In the ruin
Of green caves
Caverned out by
The toppling
Sea's wall; next, left

Almost stranded
In the slack smooth
Silk of the
Spent water's
Sucking out – till, breath
Drawn, the sea
Swells up
Once again, leans

Forward, looming
Large, and falls

Upon them, sending
A runner of thin water up
Again at me
To catch
Me by the feet.

*

Strung along the
Shore are
Shells, stranded in
Small drifts – stains –
On the sand; like
The treasures of a
Sunset
On the sky. Looking

Downward at
My feet
I am back again
In childhood, gathering shells
(This time though, these
Are for my
Grandchildren): from which

I have not stirred. No
Rarer, finer thing
I'll ever

Know than
What I found – than
What I felt – once
On my home
Sea shore as a
Solitary
Small boy (walking then,
As I do now upon
This African
Sea shore, the shore of
The sea-edge
Of our

Human understanding): the

Sharpened
Long tower of
A spiral
Whelk shell, fine as a
Pencil, up which,
Added to
The architecture, ran
Ribs I had
Never seen before
On any
'Castle' shell, as we
Called

Such shells (they were
Very much like shells
I find here
Occasionally
Among the others, but
Here these are
Thicker, wider at
The base, at once
More homely
And more outlandish). That
Shell is

What I am
Looking for
In life; and seek in
Death too, out, out
From this shore –
Away, dark there –
In the sea.

Here also
Are other translations of
Shells I
Knew at home. Cockles,

Diminutive as
Kittens, as a baby's

Hand: each line
Of the adult shell
Being marked exactly
On a shell which,
Almost transparent, is
Smaller than your
Little finger nail. And

Larger cockles: thick
However – and some of
Them with
A hole worn through the
Substance of
The nose, where the rays
All draw
Together, convenient

For hanging from a
Neck thread (for my
Granddaughter
Aged three). And other

Bivalve mollusc
Shells, fragile, flat –
An asymmetrical
Oval
Over an inch and
A half in
Breadth – tinged pink or
Reddish within the
Thickness of the lime.

Seals – all these – set on
Something. A clear
Final statement: a still silent

Summing up (which
You can
Pick up, take away
With you) of
The size and sounding
Violent
Motion of the sea.

*

Some shells have on
Them a small black
Patch: of – what
Is it? Tar?

Crude oil,
Evidently. The
Soles of my feet, I
Find, are
Stuck with it. There is
Some between two
Toes. And now

I see small
Pellets of
This, black,
Everywhere, washed up
Among the rest
Of the thin
Jetsom.

The innocence
Of the sea's
Fresh salt and
Of washed sand is thus
Sullied

Doubly: from the
Sea as well as
From the land; by village ancient
Excrement, and by our

New world – tankers, dumping
Crude oil, somewhere
Away off shore.

One picks one's
Way, as best
One can, among these
Opposite
Simultaneous evils: as,

In other
Contexts, one does
Elsewhere
In the world.

        *

Stranded, high
Up, opposite
The middle of the village
Is a felled
Tree trunk, eight feet thick
And a dozen paces
Long: like some
Weighty piece
Of the earth's
Machinery – its use
Unknown – worked
Loose
By the sea. A few

Villagers are at
It: prizing
From it
Firewood – using
Adzes and a
Blunt axe. A woman

Among them, mounted on
The top, against the
Sky line, as if
On a mountain, heaves up her
Heavy adze above
Her head, against the sky, and
Brings it down in
A full
Swing – her head
Down, forward from the waist –
Like the falling
Of a wave: her weighing
Breasts,
Full, pendulous,

Swinging forward
With the motion (a
Breaking wave that
Buries one in
Pleasures), exposed
Inside the opening of
Her thin
Shift. Below,

A man hacks
With his axe – till another
Woman, with an
Adze, can splinter
A small
Chip off. The operation

Is as slow yielding, as long,
Laborious, as the
Labour of the sea.

On the shore above – above
The earth-filled
Blackness
Of the dry loose
Sand – are idle
Coconuts: rounding out (full
Of a cool, sweet
Water) high at the
Unfolding centre
Of the tree tops'
Tuft
Of leaf fronds.

The heavy
Welling of the waves – the sway
Forward of the working
Woman's breasts, against the
Sky line – the round
Youth of
The coconuts, light green,
Which cluster high
Up there

For us (promise of what
May – when brought
Down, yielded, to
Us – be pressed
Against the lips): this
Is a
Heavy, kindly
Shore; full of
Reward, treasure –
Meaning. The sea

Itself is
Put into one's hands.

*

Against the blank
Of sea and shore

Is written
In spare
Characters, clear as those
Sea shells – in
One brief
Statement then another – the
Significance of
Things: as it
Were in
Silhouette. As

That woman is on
The log's hill
Against the sky.

Significance – untranslatable –
Is from the origin
Of things; and leads
You direct to
It: away
From words
And our world, away from

That life we lead in
Which, with an absorbed
Solemnity, we play our
Children's games, acting
Out our
Fantasies, our compulsions and
Obsessions, creating thus

A universe
To live in in the
Shape of
Us – convinced meanwhile

That this is
Necessity, fate, is what's
Imposed upon us by
Society, nature, God.

On this shore
I escape from
That. Here, for a
While, in part,
One gets
Out of prison. Small

Wonder – since
One side of the world is
Taken down: there, out
To sea.

On that pure
Substance, meaning
Itself
Is said.

5

Where a sandy lane
Through the huts
Emerges from the
Village, groups of people are
Standing on the shore, beside

A shelter or two where
Squatting men
Are darning
Fishing nets, shaded
From the sun, and fishing

Boats (heavy dugouts,
Cut from a single
Tree trunk) and hauled
Up on the

High
Shelf above the tide.

*

Walk up
The lane inland
And you find the day
Alive with
Events you do not

Understand. A band

Of dignitaries, a small
Retinue behind
Them, are pacing
Slowly forward on a route
Between the huts – two men with
Gourd-rattles sedately at
Their head – about some
Solemn business.

While further, out on the
Main road (where
Here and there

A narrow pulpit – painted
White and in
Lively innocent
Bright colours, and entwined
With animals and
Angels – is raised
Up, empty now,
Above the dirt
Upon a twisting
Flight of stairs), a

Man
Carries high upon his
Shoulders an African wooden
Image, black, a few
Feet high, of
A mother with her
Baby at the
Pointed breast: a white
Cigarette stuck for
Some reason in
Her mouth – anachronistic in
That face's black
Strict antique
Geometry. He strides

Fast, across the road –
A rabble of people
After him, awash with
Running children – toward an
Enclosed, perhaps partly
Public compound
At the other
Side: in which
No doubt some
Rite, some service, will
Be held. Ignorance, above

All of these
Languages, cuts
Me off.

The image, and its
Followers, are
Foreign – someone standing

Near by
Tells me: from
Ghana. And that

Is all
I am
Able to discover.

*

On the shore, beside the
Boats, a score or so
Of men and boys
Are hauling
On a rope – pulled

By it
Down the shore as each
Great wave
Goes out, and hauling it
Up, each time
A little further, as the
Next wave
Rushes in – in

A tug-of-war apparently
Against the
Sea itself. They line

The rope right
Down to the water, and
Mass about the
End of it up
On the high
Shelf above
The tide line; while

One of them is
Down in the waves'
Green trough
Tugging at the
Net – with
Its floats – at
The rope's
Sea end. As each wave

Flattens and draws
Out he wraps yet
Another length
Of wet heavy
Net about the rope's
Tautness, with a heave – to

Be immediately
Drowned by the next,
Overwhelmed by
Chaos, his black head
Bobbing like a cork.

Gradually the
Long rope is hauled
In, into
A heap, and next the
Net – narrowing to
A bag-shape
As it (and the
Floats that
Hold it – seen
Now twenty
Yards out) are
Steadily pulled in.

Beyond, fishing
Boats are laying more
Nets – each in a wide
Half circle – out
On the smooth
Far blue.

Beside me, a man
Hauling on
The rope – middle aged,
Square, short and amiably
Ugly – breaks into
Conversation (in uncertain
French at first,
Then English when I
Find he
Comes from Ghana). There'll

Not be a good
Catch, he says,
Till after
Four o'clock,
When the moon
Rises. He goes on
Heaving at the net. All

Of a sudden
Like a cork
It's lightened and
With a rush comes
Up the sand: its

End a
Sack – filled
With a little
Leaping
Silver. The net's

Folds are
Parted, opened: and there
Lie a heap of
Mackerel – living,
Silvery as
The moon – several

Jellyfish, sprats of
Some sort, and a crab or
Two: a few
Bucketsful. No
Catch at all.

However, this is
Divided up,
According to some
Equitable
Principle or other, among the
Tug-of-war men, people standing
By and busy
Hovering children, and carried

Away, in buckets, baskets or
The hand. And the

Net's again
Got ready: to load
Into one of
The waiting
Dugouts (built
Up a little
At the upper
Edge with extra
Patching timber) beached
High, dry: like hounds

On a leash, their
Prow
Pointing out to sea.

Perhaps after
Four o'clock the
Catch will
Be better. Seagulls

Are flying
Far out, on the right, and
Coming closer: none
Near the cast
Nets, or in shore – that
Is not where
The shoals are.

Behind the scenes of the
Daylight world we
See – beneath
The sea's
Surface, spread
Out clear before
Us – fish
Shoals
And the moon
Are: moved by
Their own
Laws. And we,

On our shore
Here, try to
Catch their phosphorescent
Moonlight
In a net. By which

Nourishment – material,
Yet mysterious as
Manna – we
Survive, under the blue
Bank of the sky. As this
Fishing village
Does at
The sea's edge.

6

Beyond the village,
Toward a
Bathing beach – a couple
Of miles off – for
The rich and Europeans, the
Excrement
Decreases; and the oil

Nodules, with
This change of
Epoch, appear to
Be more frequent.

A small boy and
Later a young
Woman, seeing what
I am doing,
Start industriously,
Obligingly, picking up
Sea shells
For me. I wish they
Would not! What I

Want's not
Shells, but – in blank
Absence of mind, open – to
Come upon shells
Here and there
That please me
And, if I feel
Like it, perhaps
Pick them up. How

Explain this, without a
Common language (they have
No French) or even,
If we had one,
With it? I have some
Difficulty in
Escaping, without incivility

Or a banal
Sackful.

Then a youth
Overtakes me, producing
A leather
Model of a Sahara
Camel saddle, which he
Wants to sell. (What
Should I do with
That?) He's

On his way evidently
To the European
Beach: motorcars
And money. He tells

Me he is half Sahara
Tuareg, and half
French – and looks
It: rather pale, with
Flattish features, quite
Un-negro. He has to

Support himself – and his
Sister, illegitimate, as
He is – by
Making saddles, like
This one

That I don't
Want. I give him a
Hundred francs or so and
Wish him luck – since,
Looking him in the eye, I
See

Someone within.

His sister, he says, is
Whiter even than
He is. Won't I

Come back with him
To his hut and
Let them
Entertain me? I say I'd

Be delighted to, and
To meet his
Sister; and thank
Him: but I do not
Have the time (indeed I
Do not – I'm here to
Be alone!) And
Anyway, as to his
Sister, I am

Married – already have
A wife. Here, in
Abidjan? Well, no:
In England. I see I am
Expected to have an

African wife as
Well, for my stay's
Duration. Their father –
Who disappeared into the sky
Like Jove, in an aeroplane –
After all
Did. We part

With a frank
Uncomprehending
Handshake.

The boy has an
Aristocratic upstanding
Independence – from
Those slave-owning Tuareg
Aristocrats on his
Mother's side I
Imagine, rather than
From that
Equivocal French
Father, by whom he was
He was
Abandoned. I like

Him: so far as I can
See behind his eyes.

Having shaken off
Thus – with sufficient
Politeness – his insistence

I sit
And become blank
Looking out to sea.

*

Every now and then a
Wave more
Dynamic than the others
Washes high
Up the shore – obliterating
The holes in which
Small crabs are
Living: that open

Up again
Immediately after. The

Crab – transparent, up
To a couple of
Inches long – creeps
To the edge
Of the hole and, if
All's
Still, darts
Out suddenly
A foot or more
To catch some
Prey or other: invisible. And
Shoots back, plock,
Into the hole – as quick as
Snapped elastic. Then

Waits again
At the hole's
Crater edge.

Other small
Holes open. Other
Sorties are made, quicker almost
Than the eye can
Catch. And again
The whole scene

Is blotted out
By an
Expunging wave.

Over the sea, in shore,
White sea
Birds are flying
Just beyond the breakers.
One

Drops: and I expect
It – like
The seagulls I am
Used to – just to
Dip
Beak, then feet, in the
Water, with a wide
Flapping of wings, and
Skimming
Fly on. It does

Not. Dropping
Down, like
A stone – instead of
Drawing up, back,
Checked, then
Winging on – it

Accelerates as it nears the
Surface of the water
And dives

Through it, in,
Down, like
A sword thrust – a blow

Silent
At its point of
Impact – without
Splash or ripple, and

Vanishes. The glass pane
Of the surface does not
Break, white:
Nothing happens. The sea is
As it was. And there is

No bird
Above it.

Again, another
Does
That. A moment or
Two later, some yards
Away from where it
Dropped
Like a plummet
In, there it

Is again, reappeared
On the surface, without
Preliminary, from
Nowhere, from
The underwater utter
Other world
Of absence – a fish

Caught, from the
Shoal beneath,
No doubt – and flies
On. Never before

Have I seen
Gannets. They are making
Along the shore toward
The fishing nets; the moon

It seems
Has brought the
Shoals in.

Reversal suddenly of
The order
Of things (the breath
Stops, and there is
Space, a hole, nothing
Where the
Heart
Was): revolution! – as,

Clean as a knife, straight
As a dropped
Stone, the bird, not swoops
Upon, but
Stabs into
The water: no
Longer is, is
Gone!

Gannets, and the crabs,
Are written
Sharp, full of meaning
And without
Explanation, on the clear
Sheet of this
Sea shore.

At length, filled
With the folding
Movement, the change
And stillness, force and
Wide high
Quiet of the sea – become

Pellucid down to the
Inmost centre
Of myself from which
Is seen, in its
Particularities, the extent
Of things, the entire
Sweep of the sky and
The horizon – I

Shake myself: wake, move on.

*

Already there are
African families
Camped along the
Shore – alighted
From motorcars beyond
The palms or from a
Rare bus out
From the town – and

The first Europeans
I have seen
Here: distressingly
Uncomely (perhaps it's
Just that their
White skins make them
Look
Disharmonious – but I
Doubt it).

Set back on the
Tideline shelf is
A low cliff
Of peaty soil, formed
By centuries of growing
Coconuts – comfortable

To lean
Against and casting
Partial shade, as I
Sit down once
More and let the

World, changed
Again a little, settle
Round me.

Small whelk
Shells are

Embedded in the bank,
Like those along
The shore, but more
Finely coiled and
Sharper: left
By what

Earlier seas? None
Of this sort are
Washed up now on the
Salt, pale
Sand. Wash off

The brown-black
Peat upon them and
They appear
Fresh almost
As the others – although
Already half way
To being
Fossils: back in the

Slow earth's dense
Amalgam of
Past time.

Coconuts are growing
Still, above,
In a dense
Grove – extending
Back to where
The land
Sinks down and a

Shallow
Lagoon spreads, full of young
Africans bathing. A still
Blue lake – of leisure, of holiday,
Of pleasure – among
The coconuts: fed by
Rare waves
From the extreme

Highest tides.

On the fibrous ground
Beneath the trees,
In sun-slashed
Shade, coconut sellers
Sit beside mounds of
Smallish
Coconuts – just
Cut down unripe from these
Trees – among piles of
Husks and chippings. They

Slice off
The top of a young
Nut – still
Embedded tight in the
White thick flesh
Of the husk – with

A knife
For you. You
Drink. Then they

Split it – and you scoop,
With a chip of the
Husk, the young
Sweet thin
Jelly of
The meat out.

Nothing in life
Is fresher than that
Concealed
Cool pool
Within – in the dry

Day's heat. Like a
Well, cool
In the earth, or the darkness
Of an eye's
Unfathomable
Pupil, it seems to

Have no
Bottom: though you hold
The fruit's ball, small,
Complete there
In your hand. Here

Is the very
Innerness of things: never
Opened to the objective
Outer light till,
Almost, it is

In you, is
You: drunk.

7

The day
Narrows its
Net and the light
Draws in. I make

For the road.

Cars, homing to
Abidjan, pass
Me on the long
Stretch back
Across the flatness (I
Had hoped there might
Be a
Bus) to

The crossroads
Where the cattle and the
Crowds are.

Already the sky's
Architecture
Crumbles; colours
Are loose
That are not
Of the day: dangerous
Strong greens upon
The vegetation – and veils of
Uncertain sepia cast,
Powdery, equivocal, out
Across the air.

Soon
Behind me, westward, the
Sky becomes a sheet
Of orange, and
High pink, above
The palms and
Mounds of
Darkened vegetation

Massed along the shore – while
To the east is
Darkness: the advancing

Dark blue of the
Night sky.

There is a sense
Of end, of
Urgency – confusion,
Crisis. In

The bare trampled area
Round the crossroads
Lights of cars and lanterns
Are everywhere
About me, in a
Half light and half
Darkness in which,
Nothing seen
Distinctly, all appears
Far off and
Near at
Once (as though
Space itself,
Decayed, no longer fixed
And solid, had become
A disconcerting
Thing of abrupt
Faults, dangerous fissures), full of

People crowding to
Catch town
Buses, private buses, taxis
Even – all of which
Are already
Crammed – as

Everyone, packing the darkened
Landscape here along the
Roadside, tries to get
Back to town before
Night quite
Extinguishes the guttering

Familiarity of
Day.

Waiting for
A bus still, now in the
Almost complete
Dark, among the black
Storm of milling
Agitated people – chaos,
Abandonment – I might
Be, all bearings lost,
Far out at
Sea, alone in
An open boat.

At last – how many
Sea horizons
Later? – a bus
Takes me
Back, uncomfortably,
To where I
Set out
From. Changed.
Unchanged.

And a new wave
Forms in
Night's black
Sea, with its
Never to be netted
Stars, as the earth
Turns – swelling
High, to

Break white,
Open,
On the morning.

AFTERWORD

by

MICHAEL SCHMIDT

Abidjan, West Africa: a place on a map, remote, strange, unromantic. Dawson Jackson travels light. His eye and his spirit are clear. He comes not as a tourist but to do a job, and the place takes him by surprise. He does not colonise it with alien expectations or appropriate its particulars in order to probe in his poem a subjective reality. The poem belongs to the world it witnesses. Its strangeness and the illumination that strangeness provides are its subject and theme. Max Plowman, writing of Jackson's 'spiritual astringency' evident in every weighed line, said of the early poems: 'Your object . . . is to express unified experience – experience in which the old dichotomy of subject and object is transcended.' The form Jackson has evolved answers the themes which have developed from the very firm givens of his early verse and prose.

'This poetry is not lyrical utterance either of the elated or dejected (Larkinesque) sort,' Charles Tomlinson wrote. 'Nor is the I in it a free-floating lyrical I. By attending to all that surrounds him – the foreignness and yet the humanity of Africa – Dawson Jackson is left free to be himself without self-regard. The lucidity of his poetry is the measure of the integrity he brings to experience. He has nothing to hide and the whole aim of his style is to make things clear. His verse offers the continuous fascination of an honest and exact diary of daily but miraculous events.'

Jackson's technique is subtle and simple. His verse form is not 'free' but (in Basil Bunting's distinction, which Donald Davie adopts) 'unmetered'. It's an insistent mode of notation, playing now with and now against the flow of syntax, like musical notation allocating time and value to different phrases and words: 'an extra system of punctuation' as he says. It denies metrical regularity at every point yet creates regularities of emphasis over long measures, at the same time indicating pace and inflection. Jackson describes enjambement as 'a slight trip effect on the eye'. Such effects register in the voice, on the ear.

But they only register if the reader allows them to. Jackson's formal approach is so against the grain of expectation, even for those readers accustomed to William Carlos Williams and the Objectivists, that his poetic takes some getting used to.

The technique makes readers proceed more slowly, though they gain the impression of speed because the lines are generally short. This curious contradiction is an inherent formal property: the poem is smooth, consecutive, yet insists on its precisions and nuances of meaning, its unpredictability. Nothing in the medium is accidental or merely mechanical, yet Jackson would like readers to read 'as if the line-breaks were not there': they are intended to produce an effect without the reader being critically aware of it.

He describes his concern in writing poetry as 'a celebration of the exactitudes of the "being so" of things' – what the early Modernists called 'the urgent, insurgent now'. 'Now' for Jackson in his poems is revelatory, with a mystical content far from the mainstream Christian in quality, uninsistently Eastern in tenor.

He is a visual writer. It is not his *images* that suggest this description. They can be and usually are descriptive rather than metaphorical in value – he might well have been a painter. He is visual too in the way he disposes lines on the page, the 'trip effect' of line breaks registers on the eye, and the stanza or paragraph breaks work in a similar manner, delivering the sense in clear, clausal units.

Among contemporary British poets Jackson stands alone. There is no contact between his work, which belongs to the generation of Spender and Auden or, stretching a point, to that of Dylan Thomas and George Barker, and the 'main stream' of modern poetry. There are apparent affinities with the American Projectivists (his poems have appeared prominently in the *New Directions* anthologies of James Laughlin), but they are accidental. When I first read his work years ago I was put in mind of William Carlos Williams, but there was a problem of diction, a sense that the language of his verse with its problematic lineation was somehow too direct. Should what he said be banal the poem would be banal. He used no tricks, no defences. He wrote boldly even when he struck what seemed a naive or over-general note. There is no more irony in Jackson's verse than in Lawrence's, though each can write humorously and satirically – and erotically – in ways which do not play to any specific audience or class; yet Jackson writes the language of his native class, and there is a curious gap between this language and his intimate, unguarded tone, a gap as wide as the one we experience in Tony Harrison, though Jackson is moving in a different social direction.

Born in Wallasey, a Wirral suburb of Liverpool, in 1910, Dawson Jackson was the second son (with a younger brother and sister) of a reasonably well-to-do family. He attended a suburban prep school, then Oundle where he excelled himself in all fields apart from Latin and Greek. He almost failed to get to Oxford on account of Latin. But at 17 he matriculated at Christ Church to read Modern History. He received a first class degree when he was twenty, having been disappointed with his literary peers (Spender *et al*). He rebelled in personal appearance and dress and set off to make his own way in the world.

The world included a woman painter somewhat older than himself with whom he had been living and then a twenty-year alliance, soon becoming marriage, with Phoebe Ashburner, poet and lecturer. His only child Unity was from this union, born in 1937. The Jackson ecology was generally sound: he grew much of the food they needed in the garden of their 'primitive' cottage. It is hardly surprising that Edmund Blunden, in 1942, wrote praising Jackson's eye for country things: 'your sense of Nature is choice in the detail. I think John Clare himself would have said so.'

To earn a living, Jackson eventually decided to learn Russian in order to translate for a friend with an ecological research bureau in Oxford. He started from scratch and taught himself enough of the language in six months to start translating: slowly – at first earning 9d an hour. 'I'm bad at languages,' he comments. 'It's amazing what economic terror will do.' And so the Jacksons survived in the more or less remote provinces – latterly in working class Northampton – until 1947. During the war Jackson was a Conscientious Objector.

In these years he wrote hard. He published in the *New Statesman*, *Adelphi* and other periodicals. Max Plowman (editing Middleton Murray's *Adelphi*), Hugh I'Anson Fausset and others encouraged him.

Jackson deliberately chose poverty, and still chooses it. A 'blazing economic and social anger' on behalf of people less advantaged than himself flared in his late teens and during the Depression, and never left him. 'One could at least join them, even if one could not help very much.'

In 1947 he took the United Nations (and later the OECD) examination and became a part-time freelance translator with international organizations abroad, translating – always on paper – French and Russian. For the next thirty years he worked some four and a half months a year – after retirement age halving that amount – for various acronymous organizations: the United Nations, WHO, FAO, UNESCO, Council of Europe, Organization of African Unity, African Development Bank, International Court of Justice, ILO, ITU, GATT, ICM . . . His work took him to India, to West, East and North Africa, New York and Washington, Peru and most of the major centres of Continental Europe, particularly Geneva. He describes it as 'scribe charlady work', but he has profited from the travel.

In 1955 Jackson married a second time, his wife being Joan Hart, a long-time companion, distinguished radio actress and writer of plays, scripts and poetry. They lived together in St John's Wood, London, until her death in 1984.

Jackson has been a writer more prolific than published. His mature work began to get written in the 1940s, culminating in the first extended undertaking, a novel-length poem called *All Is Never Said*. A second period culminated, after the war, with another novel-length verse opus entitled *The Ruin*. Since then Jackson has completed (as well as a number of miscellanies) a series of large-scale verse works: *Rome*, *New York*, *Delhi*, two African trilogies, *The Elder Brother*, *Abidjan* and *Spring Beneath the Alps*. Ironically, his bibliography of published works consists chiefly of prose titles: a novel, a philosophical meditation, and a major ecological statement, *Against Destruction*.

Max Plowman perceived early on what the absence of audience might do to a 'poet of meanings' like Jackson. In a sense he has written his verse into a void, only the smaller lyrics finding their way into pamphlets, magazines and on to radio. It is as though Rubens were known only from diminutive easel-works and miniatures. 'You do not,' Plowman wrote, 'find it easy to trust your reader to come and meet you'. In Jackson's case the absence of readership has been deleterious not only to the literary milieu but to the poet himself. Criticism, applause and censure might have sharpened the poet's sense of his receptors and led to a greater feeling of dialogue.

What I value in Jackson's poetry is the absence of irony, of obliquity. I relish the directness with which he approaches his large subjects. He will not – though no doubt he could – make his experience literary, heighten and enhance his natural language with distracting or decorative nuance. He is a Doric poet in a Corinthian age. Of an early prose book of his, E. J. Scovell wrote of the way in which Jackson's 'sight touches things so lightly and deeply at once'. This is as much a function of sight as of style.

Over the years I have become fascinated with his insistence on directness, his plain language and technique of lineation which at first struck me as a nervous tic and now seem a supple, suggestive notation, indicating at once pause and pace. Herbert Read criticised, back in 1943, Jackson's 'rhythmic atomism' and begged him to explain why he spoiled such vivid imagery and evident sensibility so deliberately. After Jackson's explanation,

Read wrote: 'the additional qualities which you aim at achieving by your line division do not compensate for the disadvantages of an eccentric form'. The form remains fresh and puzzling 45 years later. It no longer looks eccentric but expressive. Perhaps A. S. J. Tessimond, writing in 1948, was closer to the reality of Jackson's style: 'I like immensely the *cleanness* of your writing; the wiriness, the tautness; the feeling, the tenderness that aren't afraid of themselves . . .' Jackson suggests that the influence of Whitman's long lines (to which he responded warmly) led to his short lines, rather as the rich excess of Proust can occasion, in writers who admire him, a strict economy, even a formal minimalism. As well as Whitman, Jackson's points of departure included Shelley and Blake – radicals all in form and content.

Jackson's practice has been perfected over the years in the large-scale poems where his originality is given scope. In this age long poems have a limited chance of making their way unless they masquerade as novels or lyric sequences. *Abidjan* is no novel. It is not lyrical. It is a poem as lense, with no subject beyond the world it sees and celebrates in that world's terms, insofar as they are available to an Englishman who has discarded most of the prejudices of his race, and looks as if for the first time at this world.

Abidjan is one of Jackson's most luminous poems: it has a landscape, a people, a politics and a vision of their world and of the world. First drafted in long creative bursts in 1967–8, it underwent almost two decades' revision, the poet coming at it time after time 'from the outside'. The entire poem has been recast eight times. Effortless-seeming, this is an art of revision as intensive as Graves's and on a grander scale.

Abidjan and other long poems by Dawson Jackson are refreshing and troubling. They come to the reader without echoes of earlier literature. Jackson writes English – to paraphrase Edward Thomas welcoming the early poems of Ezra Pound – as though Shakespeare had never written. His diction is clear, neglecting semantic nuance. There are irruptions of the formal tones of a decently-heeled background and a good education. Generally his diction belongs, naturally, to a class and a period. Yet his poems focus so firmly on their subject that they allow the poet no facile freedom. The writing reveals a Protestant severity in the liberties the author allows himself. What is troubling – apart from an orientation I find hard to accept and which begs a degree of acceptance – is the unapologetic plainness of the approach. But Jackson's discipline is exemplary: poets and general readers cannot fail to benefit from immersion in something so clear, truthful, unadorned, unironic. He is a poet committed to his meanings.

The only advice I can proffer to reluctant readers is: read a few consecutive pages. The lines are short, and Jackson's is a language of accrual. Persistence, required by the technical unfamiliarity of the writing, is rewarded by a growing confidence in its formal properties. It's like learning to cycle, or fly: trust the vehicle, fix the eye ahead of the wheel or the plane's nose. Effort with an unfamiliar medium gives way to excitement: it works.